whatever
arises
LOVE
that

whatever arises LOVE *that*

A Love Revolution
That Begins with You

MATT KAHN

SOUNDS TRUE
BOULDER, COLORADO

Sounds True
Boulder, CO 80306

Cover design by Lanphear Design and Jennifer Miles
Book design by Beth Skelley

Printed in the United States of America

Library of Congress Cataloging-in-Publication Data
Kahn, Matt.
  Whatever arises, love that : a love revolution that begins with you /
Matt Kahn.
    pages cm
  ISBN 978-1-62203-530-4
  1. Love—Religious aspects. 2. Spirituality. 3. Spiritual life. I. Title.
  BL626.4.K34 2016
  204ʾ.4—dc23
                                        2015028249

Ebook ISBN 978-1-62203-556-4

10 9 8 7 6 5 4 3 2 1

In a world of endless questions,
love is the only answer.

MATT KAHN

Contents

Introduction

I AM HONORED to welcome you to a life-changing adventure we have been brought together to explore.

Perhaps you too have felt there is more to life than meets the eye. For most of my life, the Universe has worked through me to bring to this planet—and now to you—an invitation into a brand-new reality. When I first began my life's work, I referred to myself as a *channel* for my ability to allow a greater truth to speak through me. When a greater truth doesn't just come through in particular settings but consciously resides in the body, something extraordinary enters this world for the well-being of every heart. As I offer you everything I've been guided to share, may a truth that is deeper than the ups and downs of life emerge throughout your daily encounters.

Combining my role as a spiritual teacher with highly attuned intuitive and empathic abilities allows me to offer what is known as a *transmission of presence.* This allows you to feel transformation occurring on an energetic level, simply by reading the words I've been inspired to write.

When reading a book that is encoded with a transmission of healing energy, it's not a matter of scouring every chapter for a series of facts or conclusions; it is more like a guided tour through the unfolding of your highest potential that can activate dormant gifts and timeless remembrances as you explore each page. While the words I've provided play an important role in this journey, the real story being told is the ever-expanding experiences that come to life as the transmission is received.

In allowing the wisdom of the Universe to flow through me and fully inhabit this body, these words have chosen me to narrate a mystery that has been evolving in my life for the past thirty-eight years. Perhaps the reason I am sharing this mystery is to draw you deeper into a reality that has been calling you inward since the dawn of creation. Maybe these words signify a greater calling for you to transform every aspect of your life, so you may step forward as a lightbearer of a new spiritual paradigm.

Whether you know it or not, you have come to this planet during the most exciting time in human evolution. Just by being alive during these exhilarating, albeit intense, times of energetic expansion, you are assisting in uplifting the consciousness of Earth, as a gift for everyone who inhabits it. Maybe, on some level, you already know you are here for an important reason, in search of the guidance, clarity, and direction to help you find the relief, peace, and joy that you always hoped to find.

Those who resonate with this deeper spiritual calling are often referred to as *energetically sensitive souls*. While the soul refers to you, as a unique expression of source energy that has taken the form of a person in the world, an energetically sensitive soul is one who remembers their celestial roots. For the ones who are energetically sensitive, life celebrates a radical process of spiritual growth known as awakening.

In the past, an awakened being was revered as a prophet or wayshower for an evolving humanity. And yet, we are no longer living on a planet where only a handful of awakened ones reside. We have chosen to incarnate during a time when an entire planet is undergoing the process of awakening to fulfill the prophecies of every awake being who came before us.

While the expansion of consciousness in one individual is referred to as awakening, the spiritual evolution of an entire civilization or planet is known as *ascension*. During this time of ascension, you are either called into exploring the greater mysteries of your own existence, or you are so sensitive to the energy of the planet and the emotions of everyone else that you may not know how to function in such a heightened state of awareness.

Whether you are interested in knowing life beyond the horizon of conventional understanding; yearn to fulfill your role in the awakening of humanity; or wish to integrate your energetic sensitivities into a life of inspiration, happiness, and freedom, I have been brought here to support you in fulfilling each desire by guiding you into the ecstasy of your divine heart space. Since the highest wisdom in existence is heart-centered, the teachings that emanate through me are always rooted in the vibration of love. For an energetically sensitive soul, who may not realize how entrenched in a spiritual journey they already are, the most direct and powerful path is the road that leads you to open your heart wider than ever before.

This is why I refer to the ever-expansive energy that is waking up in so many beings as heart-centered consciousness, which is another way of describing the power of love in action. For the well-being of your journey, an endless depth of harmony, ease, and grace has been encoded throughout this book to heal every particle of your existence, at the rate in which you allow love to enter your world. Exactly how you invite love to awaken within you is precisely why you are here reading these words. As the fulfillment of your long-awaited destiny is revealed, I will also share the miraculous adventure that brought me here to be with you. Perhaps sharing what has happened in my life can offer greater comfort, clarity, and perspective for your journey ahead.

Growing up as an energetically sensitive and highly intuitive child was very confusing. Not only was I unable to distinguish between my own feelings and the experiences of others, but I never felt comfortable in my own skin until everyone else around me felt more at ease in their bodies. From counseling my friends on the playground to acting as a regular peacekeeper in my family, I was unable to have experiences independent of the reactions and responses of those around me. It was as if my own happiness was put on hold in order for me to serve the resolve of others.

To make things even more confusing, I was having vivid interactions with higher dimensional beings and seeing energies that others around me couldn't see. From timeless encounters with Jesus, without any religious or historical reference to who he was, to conversations with deceased relatives, I faced experiences I could neither understand nor deny.

When energetic sensitivity and intuitive abilities surface faster than the maturity of a person, these gifts can often be expressed as a sense of inferiority. For me, the biggest mystery was wondering, *Why can't others see what seems so obvious to me?* I remember declaring to the Universe, "If I can sense dimensions of reality that others are unable to recognize, may these abilities be used to help others discover such gifts within themselves."

The majority of my adolescence was divided between life as a teenager in a very liberal Jewish household and communicating with angels and Ascended Masters who regularly visited me in my bedroom. Each meeting was like a lucid telepathic communication where I would see, hear, and feel the conversations like a vivid daydream that was as real as any personal encounter. Although I met teachers and guides such as Jesus, Melchizedek, Archangel Michael, Quan Yin, and St. Germain, I never felt interested in learning their histories. Instead, I was mesmerized by the information they provided and soothed by the energy they embodied. Each guide carried their own unique frequency, like a distinct color of the rainbow, emanating such wise and loving energy. I instinctively knew they were here to help me.

Throughout these meetings, my intuitive abilities became heightened and refined, as I explored the infinite realms of the Universe. Although my parents were always supportive and encouraging of my experiences, I kept my encounters mostly to myself because each time I shared them with other people, I felt as though I was living on the wrong planet.

As a young adult, my connection with Archangels and Ascended Masters intensified as I was guided to deliver intuitive messages spontaneously to people I'd never met. Whether I was passing along precise instructions from the angels to strangers at the supermarket or offering deeply healing messages from the other side to shoppers at a bookstore, I was somehow being guided to deliver the exact words that brought miraculous relief into other people's lives. I had absolutely no idea how any of it was happening—and so perfectly—but because every experience always contained an undeniable feeling of love, I followed the instinct to trust and allow grace to shine through.

This willingness on my part to trust inevitably led to an even greater life-changing encounter for me with the Archangels and Ascended Masters, who had guided me throughout my life. During that meeting, they revealed themselves as agents of the Divine who represent various aspects of my future self. In seeing the Archangels, Ascended Masters, and myself as equal expressions of one eternal truth, a spontaneous awakening occurred within me.

From that point forward, a lifetime of realizations and initiations occurred in preparation for my timeless meeting with you. In celebration of a journey that has brought me so far in order to serve the blossoming of your potential, I openly share some of my most ground-breaking experiences and insights throughout the course of this book.

As a bridge between the mystical realms and the path of awakening, I am guided to provide you with the most revolutionary approach to spiritual growth so that your infinite wellspring of wisdom can be expressed through the joy of an open heart.

Throughout this book, you will hear me speak about your heart in a variety of ways. Whether talked about as your true innocent nature, your inner child, or your deepest sense of vulnerability, I am pointing your attention to the animated intelligence residing at the core of your being. At first, this may sound like the voice of your childhood, with many unresolved memories that require more patience, kindness, and care. Yet, as you stay the course, with the power of love guiding you every step of the way, the voice of your childhood merges with your adult mind to bring forth a resolution of spiritual autonomy that inspires the deepest realizations to dawn in your life.

Whether my life story matches your experiences or merely foreshadows a brand-new reality awaiting your arrival, may the following pages act as a virtual road map that leads to your greatest spiritual redemption.

Sometimes a journey of this depth and magnitude can either flip your life upside down or miraculously turn everything right side up—perhaps even back and forth from one moment to the next. No matter how uniquely your path unfolds, it is the wisdom of the Universe calling you out of the shadows of inferiority, so you can shine at full capacity for the well-being of all. Through every revelation and emotional release, I am blessed to support your journey, no matter how progressively or slowly your heart desires to open.

There are also many interactive experiences included in this book to help you anchor and integrate the energy you are receiving. Through the use of powerful healing mantras that have been created by the Universe to ensure your success, new frontiers of inner discovery can be noticed, just by repeating each line. Simply by reciting each mantra out loud, you are able to more clearly remember your eternal nature as well as fine tune your own intuitive guidance through the confirmation of your body's wisdom.

As love brings us together for an adventure, countless incarnations in the making, I intuitively draw on the insights from many past lifetimes to offer you the most integrated spiritual path. With every step forward, you will become rooted in the profound wisdom of four auspicious words: *whatever arises, love that.*

By loving what arises, you unearth the deepest understanding of the Universe in the most heart-centered way. As your heart opens, you are able to see how every circumstance and detail of life has been created only to help you grow on a spiritual level. Whether you know it or not, all orchestrations, encounters, and outcomes are created by the Universe as a way to help you expand to full capacity and realize the truth of your divine nature.

With love as your guide, you are able to explore a deeper spiritual reality within you that has been decorated as a person living in a world of others.

As you may have already sensed throughout your life, there are always reasons for your experiences greater than those that appear on the surface, even if you're unaware of what those reasons may be. But best of all, when love can be invited to work through you and respond on your behalf, you don't even need to know why things occur. All that is required is a willingness to open your heart. With every step forward into a new spiritual paradigm, you are able to celebrate the arrival of heart-centered consciousness while holding a sacred space for the ascension of Earth and the awakening of humanity.

Whether you are ready to embrace your experiences at a more intimate level or would rather celebrate your life under more favorable circumstances, the importance of cultivating unconditional love is an essential stage in the completion of your journey.

Whether manifesting a soul mate, healing the body, seeking liberation from suffering, or integrating past realizations into a fully embodied state of being, each spiritual milestone swiftly finds its way to you once love has been invited into your life.

This is the dawning of your highest potential. It is the emergence of your soul into the beauty of human form. It is the long-awaited fulfillment of your divine destiny. And for the spiritual growth of all who inhabit our magnificent planet, it is *a love revolution that begins with you.*

Many blessings for our journey ahead—this is only the beginning.

1

Beginning Your Love Revolution

A NEW SPIRITUALITY has dawned; one that acknowledges your energetic sensitivity and unravels every burden by inspiring your deepest vulnerability to come out and play. This is a heart-centered journey of infinite joy and endless self-discovery, rooted in the beauty of compassion and anchored by the embodiment of your highest wisdom. No matter what issues you hope to resolve, your objective within this new spirituality isn't to expand awareness with force, effort, or exhaustion. Instead, this will be an adventure that leads you directly into the depths of your being to the support you have always deserved. With every step forward along a heart-centered exploration, the most potent solution to any problem equally reveals the single greatest catalyst to awaken your deepest truth. As you say "yes" to this invitation, you leap to the forefront of human evolution by understanding that in a Universe of endless questions, *love is the only answer.*

For the energetically sensitive soul, looking within is not a matter of becoming more aware, but rather of learning how to be open and *accepting of how aware you already are.* In most cases, awareness is already fully present but in a state of hyperactivity that may cause you to be overwhelmed by your feelings and unable to distinguish your own experience from that of others. This can be a painful and overwhelming way to live until you learn how to transform your natural-born empathy into a masterfully honed intuitive skill set. When you are energetically sensitive, a modern-day spiritual journey is a transition from "fearing it all" to "feeling it all." In order to find the courage to face the experiences that may have overwhelmed you in the past, a set of divinely inspired instructions, transmitted by the Universe, are available to you. While only four words in length, they reveal an open heart as your only source of refuge.

These four words are *whatever arises, love that.* By learning how to love what arises, a tendency to fight with the inevitability of outcome transforms into a willingness to embrace the ever-changing circumstances of life. Throughout this process, you are relieved of the overwhelming heaviness felt in the world by returning to the ecstasy of your true innocent nature. In the new spiritual paradigm, you cannot wait for your heart to open in order to love. No matter how closed off you feel or how shut down you seem to be, it is your willingness to love that reminds you how safe you've always been.

With love as your guide, you activate the most potent form of healing to shift all areas of your reality. As healing occurs, you fulfill your journey by bringing forth a heart-centered consciousness for the well-being of all. This is why I refer to the new paradigm of spirituality as *a love revolution that begins with you.* As the love revolution unfolds, you will start to view your path not as the evolution of one among many others, but as the awakening of all—expressed into form as the expansion of an individual.

By loving what arises, the pitfalls of energetic sensitivity blossom into the grace of Spirit in action. As you become an anchor of heart-centered consciousness, seeds of transformation are planted in every corner of existence. This occurs at the rate in which *your true innocent nature* becomes the object of your affection.

Whether you are here to resolve a healing crisis, discover true joy and fulfillment, or make peace with the past, it is now time to shine as never before and to see how far your angel wings are destined to spread.

On behalf of the Universe, I welcome you home to a space you never left, to reveal an eternal kingdom that has always existed within you. As this new reality dawns, a timeless truth echoes throughout all dimensions to gently remind you:

> In every breath you take, love is always here.
> Throughout any personal encounter, love is
> always here. No matter what comes together or
> whatever is pulled apart, love is always here. In
> your greatest moment of achievement or even in
> your darkest hour of uncertainty, love is always
> here. Whether in the aftermath of tragedy
> or in the presence of your highest triumph,
> love is always here. When life is flowing,
> inspired, and harmonious, and even if it's

frustrating, annoying, painful, or inconvenient, love is always here. When you feel alone or unsupported, love is always here. No matter what you understand and despite what you have yet to figure out, love is always here. Despite your thoughts, regardless of what you choose, or how you feel, love is always here. No matter what has been done to you or whatever you believe you've done to others, love is always here.

As love is revealed, the light of your highest potential eases the overactive mind by releasing layers of emotional clutter. These are the natural results you've always been destined to receive to celebrate the true purpose you came to fulfill. Such a divinely appointed purpose helps you recognize your own heart as the center of the Universe. One heartfelt embrace at a time, all beings are blessed, uplifted, and returned to the magnificence of their original form. This is what it means to begin your own love revolution. It is an opportunity to inspire the transformation of all by cherishing your innocence as never before.

By loving what arises, you cross a life-changing threshold during the most exciting time in Earth's history. As more beings than ever before are awakening to the truth of their eternal nature, you are assisting in the spiritual growth and energetic expansion of an entire civilization, just by learning to live with an open heart. A sign that you are ready to take such an important leap is often felt as an intense calling to unravel the collective unconsciousness of humanity by healing yourself. Perhaps this calling may feel like a recurring impulse to find personal fulfillment, true liberation, and abiding peace without having to regularly rearrange the furniture of your reality. No matter the signs that signify your readiness, these words confirm that you have successfully answered the call to return to love.

Throughout this heart-centered revolution, you come to realize that underneath it all love is what you are and all you've ever wanted. The willingness to accept this truth and assist in the transformation of humanity is an essential stage of growth that I call *the eternal cultivation*. During this vital stage, your body expands into a conscious vessel of awakening by providing your innocence the encouragement, kindness, and care it has always desired.

In the most practical and approachable way, I am honored to assist you in opening your heart to release each worry, dissolve every limitation, and raise the vibration of the planet as a gift of transcendence for one and all.

Love as the Ultimate Equalizer

As you embrace yourself more sincerely than ever before, you may discover how your own heart has often been the last in line to receive the support and attention that you give to others. As your heart expands, you no longer overlook opportunities to provide yourself with the same kindness and care that so many in your life are blessed to receive. One loving embrace at a time, you become a living testimony of just how powerful, aligned, inspired, and happy you have always been destined to be.

By loving what arises, you set aside any tendency to deny, avoid, or fight with the inevitability of life to awaken the most profound intimacy within you. In honor of how far you've come, I invite you to take this moment to celebrate the arrival of a new reality.

Whether you wish to speak these words out loud or read them silently to yourself, please repeat the following healing mantra:

> When I'm sad, I deserve more love, not less.
> When I'm angry, I deserve more love, not less.
> When I'm frustrated, I deserve more love, not less. Whenever I'm hurt, heartbroken, ashamed, or feeling guilty, I deserve more love, not less.
>
> Even when I'm embarrassed by my actions, I deserve more love, not less. Equally so, when I'm proud of myself, I deserve more love, not less. No matter how I feel, I deserve more love, not less. Despite what I think, I deserve more love, not less.
>
> No matter the past that I've survived, I deserve more love, not less. No matter what remains up ahead, I deserve more love, not less. On my worst day, I deserve more love, not less.
>
> Even when life seems cruel and confusing, I deserve more love, not less. When no one is here to give me what I need, I deserve more love, not less. In remembering the greatest way I can serve the world, I deserve more love not less.

> No matter what I'm able to accept, whomever I cannot forgive, or whatever I'm unable to love for whatever reason, I deserve more love, not less.

In celebration of your true innocent nature, love doesn't ask you to accept what cannot be accepted; it simply says, "Just embrace your own heart, and I will accept on your behalf." It does not ask you to forgive what is unforgivable, but simply says, "Just embrace your own heart, and I will forgive on your behalf." It doesn't even ask you to love what cannot be loved. Instead, it simply says, "Just embrace your own heart, and I will love on your behalf."

No matter the circumstance at hand, love ensures that everything is done *through* you, instead of *by* you. By embracing your innocence more than anyone has ever dared to embrace it, you find the parent you've never met, a best friend you never knew you had, and the lover who has been there all along, as the truth of what you are. Equally so, by making your own heart the object of your affection, you invite the truth of others to be recognized beyond the characters they're imagined to be. With love as your guide, the uniqueness of all can be equally appreciated, without the pain of conflict dividing you from another.

While it is necessary to realize that others may not be able to love you in the way you have always desired, you don't have to lack the kindness, support, and care that your love revolution brings to life. Whether in the aftermath of disappointment or at the brink of despair, the depth of attention that you can provide yourself allows emotions to no longer be the lingering evidence of a painful existence. When rooted in your heart, every reaction can be viewed as a perfectly orchestrated activation of consciousness, clearing out the old paradigm to make room for something new to unfold. This often occurs at the rate in which each particular feeling is honored and given permission to be.

No matter how easily or slowly you open up to the feelings that inspire your most profound transformation, it is important not to rush the process. Instead, it is essential to take your time and make every moment count by remembering that you always deserve more support, kindness, and encouragement along the way.

No matter how daunting, overwhelming, or uncomfortable your experiences seem to be, the ups and downs of everyday life can be transformed into a deeply fulfilling spiritual adventure, simply by becoming the source of your own fulfillment.

The invitation love offers is never bound by any belief or limited by any role you happen to play. It is an invitation to merge back into the light of divinity by remembering those four words that call out to you: *whatever arises, love that.*

Through a willingness to love more often, you are able to remember the deeper spiritual reasons for why circumstances occur. Beyond beliefs in superstition, every moment is created by the Universe to ensure your highest growth. The fact that you experience discomfort is only evidence of how rapidly you are expanding. In an effort to make your adventure as rewarding and joyful as possible, we have been brought together to remember how exciting change can be once your heart has been given permission to open. With love leading the way, each feeling and circumstance can be celebrated as an activation of expanded consciousness.

As you make peace with the sudden discomfort or lingering pain of your personal frustrations, a greater perspective allows you to view life through the eyes of the Universe instead of feeling stuck as a person within it. No matter what seems to trigger you, each reaction represents the releasing of cellular debris collected from lifetimes of experiences. When your heart is open, you are able to notice that *anything* you are feeling is part of a healing taking place within you. Conversely, when your heart remains closed, the emotions you sense always seem to be viewed as barriers to your highest fulfillment.

Learning to Love What Arises

Throughout this process, it is important to remember that a sensation only feels like a barrier for as long as you refuse to feel it. As it is invited to be felt, a willingness to experience each moment as an opportunity to heal clears out layers of cellular memory to make room for the emergence of heart-centered consciousness.

For many people, it's easy to judge those uncomfortable feelings that always seem to erupt at the most inconvenient moments. The more often such feelings are triggered, the more effortless it becomes to interpret each surge of emotional reaction as an ongoing problem that has to be fixed. You can even seek out countless healing modalities, or various spiritual paths, hoping something will make the distracting, painful, and inconvenient nature of feelings disappear. While a path or healing process can offer you momentary relief through reframing or changes of state, the feelings inevitably come back until you are able to acknowledge each reaction as evidence of a deeper journey already in progress.

While many become disheartened and frustrated when the promise of a modality or spiritual path doesn't live up to its claims, through the eyes of the Universe it is obvious that nothing can take away the proof that profound healing is underway. Your highest wisdom invites you to see every reaction as a moment of spiritual activation. Through the welcoming of any feeling, cellular debris is released out of your energy field. Since each individual is an expression of the Universe, the cellular debris released out of one person simultaneously assists in the healing of all.

This is why loving what arises is the single most important way to fulfill your divine destiny. One heartfelt embrace at a time, you are able to welcome the spontaneous healing that shifts your reality and supports the evolution of every being—all at once.

Like children tugging at the pant leg of a parent, each emotional reaction reminds you of the perfect moment in time to participate in your healing journey. By acknowledging the deeper healing that occurs when allowing each emotion to be openly felt, you have already taken your first exciting step toward loving what arises. The farther you go, the easier it is to make peace with the perfectly orchestrated catalysts that can often make your life seem out of control. The more each feeling is welcomed, no matter how uncomfortable or inconvenient it seems to be, the easier it is to be aligned with your heart—despite the circumstances in view.

While many people acknowledge love as a noble value and even recognize it as the highest vibration in existence, very few are aware of how to love without being inspired by the actions of another. It can be easy to reciprocate when you are on the receiving end of compliments from your partner, and it is natural to find the innocence of animals and children endearing. However, for many, the very remedy their heart cries out for—love—seems elusive because they do not know how to cultivate it by offering it freely.

Once you allow feelings to be felt on a more intimate level, the next step is learning to relax your body. While you may not feel relaxed in response to the emotional waves that churn within you, notice what happens when you relax everything around the emotion you feel. An easy way to relax your body is to slow your breath. Many people attempt to deepen their breath but wind up inhaling quickly along the way. The key is slow, gentle breathing to remind your body it is safe to let in and feel what could only be another moment of transformation.

Once the intensity of a strong emotion is welcomed in with slower breaths, the next step is to locate the feeling you are sensing. While there can be a tendency to label each feeling in an attempt to trace it to a root cause or childhood trauma, such processes are geared more toward psychoanalyzing your memories, which can reframe your experience without healing it on a cellular level.

When only love can make it safe enough to face what you feel, the deepest healing is accessed by welcoming each sensation, without a need to analyze, contemplate, or process your experiences any further. Just by bringing greater attention to the part of your body where strong emotions or physical pain linger, you are loosening each layer of cellular memory to assist in another moment of healing. Perhaps instead of thinking about your feelings or focusing on who is to blame for your circumstances, you can choose to locate the part of your body where you notice such sensations. Once you've located this place within your body—whether it feels centered in your head, stomach, chest, or any other part of your body—simply allow your attention to rest in the center of it. If you are unsure where the feeling is located, always choose your heart as a central point of focus.

In whatever way is most comfortable for your experience, notice what happens when you allow your attention to rest in the center of any feeling by slowly breathing into it. Can you notice that the more intimately emotions are explored, the more easily they seem to disippate?

The next step in your healing journey is remembering and affirming the intention of the Universe. No matter how often you judge any reaction, your highest purpose is for every emotion to be recognized as an opportunity to return to love for the healing, awakening, and transformation of all. To help shift the insufferable nature of human conditioning into a spontaneous moment of healing, please repeat the following healing mantra:

> I accept that this feeling is only here to be
> embraced as it's never been embraced before.

When you recognize that the intention of the Universe is to invite whatever reaction, event, outcome, or circumstance that ensures your greatest spiritual discovery, you are able to reduce the sharpness of feelings and benefit from each emotional release.

As the war against discomfort and inconvenience is unraveled by accepting your experiences as contributions toward a more evolved humanity, you are able to view the activity of your life in a more spiritually aligned way. This can help you recognize even the most insurmountable odds as gateways into new paradigms of consciousness that do not require you to suffer when loving what arises.

When you remember a wise and loving Universe has orchestrated your life to inspire your highest potential in physical form, you are able to more freely offer yourself the support you need during moments when it matters the most. This can be as simple as finding a comfortable place to sit and closing your eyes while your hand rests on the location of an uncomfortable feeling. As you gently breathe your attention into the center of any feeling, simply repeat the following healing mantra, either silently or out loud:

I love you.

In a soft, supportive, and gentle tone, continue saying "I love you" like a lullaby that you would sing to a child. The more playful you allow each "I love you" to be, the more your heart will open.

Try offering "I love yous" for a two-minute period. Even if the reaction dissipates after the first few, continue to offer love as a way of reminding your innocence:

When healing occurs, and even beyond the
releasing of emotional debris, you deserve
more love, not less.

This reminds your innocence of your role as its wise and loving guardian. With more attention given to whatever arises, your true innocent nature learns that it doesn't need to be in constant crisis or emotional peril in order to receive the support you are now willing to offer.

If a reaction returns, repeat the process for another two minutes.

Whether you are experiencing constant upheavals of emotion or reveling in the large gaps between each reaction, the point isn't to be in a space where no feelings arise. Instead, you are allowing the grace of love to transform how you relate to your lifetime of experiences.

When rooted in your heart, human reactions contain an essential spiritual role, both in your personal journey and throughout the evolution of humanity. One "I love you" at a time, the perfection of divine will offers you opportunities to accelerate your healing through your willingness to embrace your heart like a child in pain. No matter how the child in your heart is feeling—fearful, agitated, sad, grieving, guilty, jealous, angry, hateful, or hurt—when returning to love becomes your primary response, each emotion acts as an invitation into a more spiritually aligned existence.

Perhaps each feeling reminds you of a time in your life when you didn't receive the attention and support you so deeply desired. One "I love you" at a time, you can offer the one who remembers the past that shaped your view: the kindness, support, acceptance, and care that allows the influences of human conditioning to be resolved. By embracing your feelings with heart-centered attention, you are equally helping to dissolve patterns of judgment throughout the collective unconscious.

This may help you acknowledge so-called "negative" experiences as remarkable expansions in evolution. Even if confronted by an emotion that is too difficult to face or feels impossible to love, this simply becomes an opportunity to love the one who is unable to openly face the fate of their experiences.

Like a processional line of cosmic redemption, each moment of healing brings to the surface layers of emotions that await your embrace. Each one represents moments from the past, where your feelings or experiences may have been judged as bad versus good.

Whether loving the one in pain, honoring the one who is scared, or acknowledging the one who refuses to face discomfort, loving what arises helps you unearth a greater cosmic picture, even in the most subtle or uneventful moments of life. Sometimes it may be difficult to believe, but everything in reality only seems the way it is so that you can recognize it as an invitation to harmonize with the light of divine will. In fact, there is no other reason that something would come into view, no matter where the finger of blame tends to point.

With every step forward along a heart-centered path, you are able to clear away the confusion by acknowledging the most pivotal reason that anything emerges to the forefront of your life. Beyond the outdated beliefs that your thoughts create your reality or are karmic punishment for past indiscretions, each emotional surge invites you to welcome in yourself all that has yet to be faced, acknowledged, or honored by anyone else.

In the most honest and intimate way, you are able to resolve every conflict that has been stored in cellular memory and projected into appearance as the world around you. Whether it seems easy at times, or impossible to approach, always trust in the power of love to make things right on your behalf.

Being Worthy of Love

As you become more receptive to your feelings than ever before, it is normal to wonder if you are worthy of receiving this much focused time and attention. Perhaps you're not feeling the love or it seems inauthentic to say "I love you" so often. Maybe you are accustomed only to hearing words of praise as a sign that you've done something right. It's natural not to know how to let encouragement in if it has been given only as a reward for good behavior. It is also understandable to push away love when it is associated with those who have hurt you.

Even if the words "I love you" have been offered by those who betrayed, hurt, abused, or abandoned you, it is imperative for you to embrace your own innocence as a way of recognizing that attention doesn't have to lead to pain, manipulation, or rejection.

With the utmost respect for every tragedy and insufferable environment, each of us has been given the power to survive; may every step forward guide you out of the ashes of a painful past to make peace with love even if you're unwilling to forgive those who have hurt you. Whether hurt, heartbroken, or hopeful, it is not uncommon for loving yourself to seem like such a new experience that your subconscious mind has no reference point for it.

The subconscious mind is comprised of two basic categories: the "familiar" and the "foreign." If, in your early history, self-love was a rare occurrence, these newer, heart-centered experiences become filed in the foreign category. As you begin to love your heart, any lack of authenticity or resonance is simply your subconscious mind's way of saying, "You haven't done this before." Since you may not have taken the time to cherish yourself on a regular basis, you are starting your own love revolution to change the way your subconscious mind responds to being the center of attention.

Every time you send love to your heart, it gets subconsciously recorded as a vote of familiarity. Even just one "I love you" acts as a precedence-setting moment once you are able to honor yourself unlike any other time in the past.

As "I love you" becomes one of the most popular phrases you either say to yourself or send as a blessing to others, your subconscious mind is rewritten to recognize love as a familiar experience.

Over time, what once fell under the category of foreign has now moved over to the category of familiar. When this shift occurs, the subconscious mind gives your body permission to resonate with love as a fully embodied experience of truth. As your subconscious mind becomes more acquainted with love, you are able to sense the validation, safety, and security that you may have thought always needed to come from others.

Each time you are able to love what arises, you are not only releasing cellular debris out of your body but unraveling judgments out of your subconscious mind. The more judgments are unraveled throughout this process, the easier your heart is able to remain open.

Simply by repeating the phrase "I love you," you become the source of your own fulfillment, while rewriting your subconscious mind with consistency, patience, and ease.

As you resonate with love as a truthful and more familiar experience and feel safe enough to let life in, you are able to provide love to others as a profound gift of transformation. Whether through compliments, acts of kindness, deeper eye contact, or even a simple smile, to the degree that your innocence is embraced, you can provide the same to others.

When opening your heart is acknowledged as one of the greatest contributions you can make, you further your journey by inviting love to evolve our planet. From this space, you can recognize true healing as a willingness to treat yourself and others better than you were ever treated in the past.

Rewriting the Subconscious Mind

One of the most important steps in loving what arises is learning how to rewrite your subconscious mind. By allowing "I love you" to become a familiar phrase that you offer to yourself on a regular basis, love is no longer interpreted as a foreign invasion.

Simply by treasuring your heart more often, you provide your body the much-needed permission to receive the highest vibration in existence that only love can deliver. With your body calibrated in greater resonance, you access an innate ability to change all past associations to love that may have influenced you to have a painful or skeptical view of it. Such resonance also informs your immune system how to act since the body tends to function as a living expression of the most popular phrase recorded in your subconscious mind.

With love as your remover of obstacles, delivering frequencies of light into every aspect of your being, you are assisting in the awakening of the world, simply by daring to shine more brightly. By being on the receiving end of your own emotional support, you allow the innocence in every heart to end all fights, heal each wound, and surrender every judgment.

As is true with any spiritual path, it is natural to notice a tendency to push yourself faster than your innocence is ready to respond. This of course creates more discord and causes your heart to stay closed instead of opening up. In order for your heart to blossom, it must be given the right to open as quickly or slowly as it desires. If this creates a stir of impatience or panic inside, it can become an opportunity to recognize the one who feels this way as the next one in line to be loved. Whatever arises in response to your experiences, which can include no response at all, shows exactly where love can be sent.

This allows loving what arises to be one of the most unique and foolproof paths in existence because even the feedback that you interpret as "this isn't working" could only be another perfectly orchestrated moment of healing underway.

Whether your feedback reveals "the one who feels like a failure," "the one who can't get it right," "the one who has no control," or even "the one who never gets their way," each one of these invites you to locate such feedback in your body.

With a soft nurturing voice, can you allow each one to be loved as they have never been loved before? If not, can you accept this as an opportunity to embrace the one who can't?

While your innocence opens up in exactly the way that ensures the evolution of your journey, there is another way to give your inner child permission to open. As a way of offering your heart the approval, support, and encouragement it needs to come out of hiding, please repeat the following healing mantra:

I don't know how to love the sadness I feel.
I don't know how to love the fear I sense.
I don't know how to love the jealousy I notice.
I don't know how to love the pain I'm in.
I don't know how to love the judgments I have.
I don't know how to love the struggles I face.

I don't know how to love the past I remember.
I don't know how to love the people who hurt me.
I don't know how to love those who ignored me.
I don't know how to love those who punished me.
I don't know how to love those who abused me.
I don't know how to love the resistance I feel.
I don't know how to love the doubt I sense.
I don't know how to love the darkness within me.
I don't know how to love the things I hate
    about myself.

I don't know how to love what's here to
    be loved.
I don't know how to love what I may never
    be willing to love.
I don't know how to love the one who can't
    seem to shift.
I don't know how to love the one who doesn't
    want to forgive.
I don't know how to love the one who refuses
    to grow.
I don't know how to love the one who always
    thinks they're right.

I don't know how to love the one who always
seems victimized.
I don't know how to love the one who believes
they're entitled at the expense of others.
I don't know how to love the one who is always
in need.

I don't know how to love the one who is always
desperate, lonely, and never fulfilled.
I don't know how to love the one who's never
satisfied and always needs more.
I don't know how to love the one who's afraid of
having less.
I don't know how to love the one who always
thinks there's something to earn.
I don't know how to love the one who just
wants to go home.
I don't know how to love those who have denied me.
I don't know how to love the one who has
always been denied.

I don't know how to love the one who always
feels unworthy.
I don't know how to love the one who chases
desire, only to push away all that is given.
I don't know how to love all that I am.

By acknowledging that I don't know how to
love, I relinquish each conflict, burden, and
hardship by entering the heart of surrender.

Please take a moment to feel the effects of this healing mantra. It might seem counterintuitive to confess the depths of what you don't know or what you don't know how to do.

And yet, in your body, there might be a profound amount of spaciousness, relaxation, and relief as a result of each confession. As you accept what you don't know, the Universe within you that knows and does it all is called into action. In response to such a mantra, the Universe resolves through you what only the grace of your honesty can ever set free.

One reaction, confession, and "I love you" at a time, you liberate yourself from a painful past to clear out your subconscious judgments and allow love to enter your world.

Even if you are unable to face certain feelings or say "I love you" for whatever reason, your healing journey expands by confessing what you don't know how to do. It's never wrong not to know how to do what you don't know how to do. It could only be the next thing to confess as a way of softening the edges of your reality.

Honoring Your Innocent Nature

Maybe you're already feeling the profound effects of becoming the source of your own loving attention. Are you able to sense how much lighter you feel when honesty is embraced at a much deeper level? No matter what your experience happens to be, everything can be seen as a powerful sign of how quickly life evolves once you reunite with the beauty of your innocent nature.

At times, you may be aware of your innocence in the aftermath of disappointment, in the presence of insurmountable change, or throughout the turbulence of unavoidable pain. Since everything is precisely orchestrated by the Universe, it is not as if you are being punished or hurt when you come in contact with these uncomfortable feelings. Soon, you may be able to see that each climate of circumstances has been assembled only to bring you into deeper communion with the feelings of your inner child. Often, it is through discomfort that your innocence is heard the loudest.

It is natural to develop an aversion to feeling difficult emotions if you're aware of your vulnerability only during moments of adversity. Maybe when you were the most open about your feelings, this led to judgment, ridicule, rejection, or even punishment from adults who became frustrated with their inability to address your concerns or change how you felt.

There might even be a sense of "if only I kept my feelings to myself, everything would've been fine." Of course, every relationship, interaction, and encounter are only brought together or ever pulled apart as catalysts of divine will in action. Although you may not receive the result you hoped for, in the end, you will look back and see every ending as the best possible outcome for everyone involved. Until then, it is essential to become reacquainted with the sensitivities of your wise and innocent heart. Perhaps it can be envisioned as the child you remember being in the past or even as the child you were never allowed to be. Whether your innocence is seen as your inner child or noticed as a raw aliveness of being, it calls out for your loving attention as a way to ensure the highest possibilities you were always meant to explore.

By making peace with uncomfortable feelings, you don't have to walk around trying so hard to feel a particular way, when in reality you're just hoping to avoid more pain and despair. It's understandable to want to avoid pain and despair, even to the extent of anticipating it on a regular basis. This is not wrong. When experienced, resistance or avoidance could only be the next one in line to be loved. Through this process, you are free to admit, "It's okay that I don't like feeling this, and yet it's here, so I can make peace with it. I recognize that the one who feels this way is like a child who never behaves the way I want them to act. No matter how this child feels, they are as deserving of my unconditional love as anyone else."

Even if you can't embrace your emotions or cherish the one who can't accept their feelings, each moment of vulnerability inspires a greater degree of honesty as your initial key to freedom. This more intimate level of honesty allows you to focus your attention on admitting what you don't know how to do, including the confession of the one you don't know how to love. As the truth sets you free, one moment of honesty at a time, the spaciousness or relief you are able to feel in your body prepares you to be receptive to love in a brand-new way. Throughout this process, it doesn't even matter how good you think you are at supporting yourself since love is a magnificent force of divine power that is cultivated by how often you invite it in.

In the new spiritual paradigm, it is essential to make peace with your emotions so you don't have to be caught in a cycle of seeking out one particular feeling and avoiding its opposite along the way. As you awaken out of a world of polarity, you are no longer tossed back and forth between the highs and lows of life. This means endless gains don't have to be followed by surprising losses simply because you have made peace with both sides, allowing either one to be an equal opportunity to love what arises. From this space of renewed freedom, bursts of joy are as valuable as overwhelming moments of despair. They may not feel the same, but both can be acknowledged as equally deserving of a love that only your heart provides.

While you cannot pretend to equally celebrate both sides of life, it is quite surprising how quickly your attitude toward circumstances can shift when your heart feels safe enough to open. With love as your guide, you are invited to make peace with the true healing purpose of painful emotions so that anything other than feeling good doesn't have to be viewed as bad. Usually, when a feeling is labeled as "bad," it suggests "this is a really bad time to feel anything other than good."

When feeling good isn't rooted in outcome or dependent upon circumstances, there is no gain or loss that comes your way for any other reason but to escort you into your next highest level of consciousness. Perhaps you experience yourself as a character who encounters endless losses just so you can be reminded of an innocence that is only here to be embraced. In an attempt to help you become more aware of this, the Universe arranges your life to bring your attention to the vulnerability that others in your past may have overlooked, ignored, abandoned, or betrayed.

Throughout your past, there may have been instances where you naturally wished the people in your life could have loved you the way you wanted to be loved. Maybe they loved you in the deepest way they could at the time, but for some reason they weren't able to provide the depth of acceptance and care that you required. Each one of these memories, in which love seemed absent from your life, is recorded in your cells. As emotions erupt, the memories that are ready to be released remind you of what it felt like during a time when you needed love the most.

As a way of answering the call of innocence, loving what arises allows you to treasure your inner child in a way that no other person may have ever done before. By allowing the spontaneous release of cellular memory to remind you of the perfect moment in time to become the best parent your innocence could ever meet, you assist in clearing more space for a new heart-centered consciousness to emerge. In essence, you are using every reaction or sensation of pain, discomfort, frustration, fear, or discord to step back in time and love yourself throughout the course of your history.

This experience helps you understand that there is a deeper meaning to being attached to your past. While many spiritual students work ferociously to relinquish attachments to past experiences, such attachments cannot dissolve until the one who grips the past has been fully accepted and adored. This also helps you recognize the cellular memory recorded throughout the cells of your body as the true meaning of karma. Many understand karma by the saying "What goes around, comes around," often stated as a suggestion of vengeance.

In truth, the experiences of childhood set the stage for you to revisit every suppressed feeling and denied memory as catalysts for spiritual growth. Seeing your feelings and memories this way not only helps you learn how to unconditionally love yourself the way no one else could, but also frees an entire planet by transforming the suffering of one into a gift of salvation for all.

Every moment of reaction is like a cross-referencing system within your cellular body. Instead of facing every single memory or needing to keep digging up the past, every feeling is like a magnet attracting all cellular memories where you felt that common emotion. For example, in a moment of sadness, the innocence within your heart says, "I bring forth all the clusters of memories when I was sad, not loved, or not supported the way I wished to be. I ask for your assistance in helping me release these clusters by loving me the way I have never been loved before."

With each heartfelt embrace, you offer your body permission to release the cellular debris that is ready to be healed, no matter the circumstances or outcomes that seem to trigger it. As always, whatever arises emotionally is already being swept out of your field. Simply by bringing your attention to the part of your body where discomfort is noticed, breathing slowly into the center of the discomfort, and responding to your inner child with gentle loving attention, you are allowing cellular debris to be moved out at a more accelerated rate.

As you take the time to reunite with your inner child, which can occur whether you are emotionally triggered or not, you become aware of a core of vulnerability that only wants you to be more attentive, loving, caring, and thoughtful than ever before. While it is both the Universe dressed up as the character you've taken yourself to be, as well as the child in your heart awaiting your support and acceptance, it is the role-playing of divine will that inspires love to come alive throughout the beauty of physical form. This reminds you that every step forward celebrates the spiritual evolution of the Universe knowing itself as the supreme innocence of all.

Although the Universe is masquerading both as a child within your heart and as the parent to this inner child, the highest destiny of divine will is for this child to emerge as the master that *you* already are. You are here on this planet going through the evolutionary process of becoming a living spiritual master, similar to the way a seed grows into itself as a fully blossomed flower. While a seed exists as the living potential of a flower, until it is planted and given permission to sprout roots, it cannot actually become the truth it has always been.

In this reunion of cosmic innocence, you are already a spiritual master who incarnated to consciously grow into the absolute potential of your true eternal nature. In order to reveal the master within you, it is essential to allow love to be your most natural response. When self-love isn't your immediate reaction, see it as an opportunity to welcome the next one in line to be supported, cherished, and embraced as never before.

A Master Revealed

EVER SINCE I CAN REMEMBER, I've always been what you would call an empath—one who is able to feel the emotions occurring in the bodies of others. While I had very advanced empathic abilities from an early age, they weren't honed and focused in any way. As a result, I was wide open, constantly feeling the energy of the world and what was unresolved in the bodies of people around me. On a regular basis, I had the innocent misunderstanding that what I felt emotionally in another person was actually their opinion of me. This led me to spending the majority of my childhood trying to cheer everyone up. For so many years, I thought changing how someone felt would allow them to like me—even though I was already well liked and could never quite accept it.

Despite everyone's efforts to offer approval and validate my existence, I couldn't truly accept that I was liked by others. This was due to a mixture of feelings I felt around people and how contrary this seemed to the words they spoke. I remember being around children and even adults who actually smiled at me, yet I always felt so much anger and sadness within them. I would often think, *Am I the cause of their sadness? Are they angry with me? Did I do something to upset them?*

Throughout my childhood, "Are you mad at me?" became the most common question I would ask. Of course, many years later, I would come to learn I was intuitively picking up on layers of emotional debris in the other person's energy field. Just like many energetically sensitive children, I spent the first phase of my life caught in a cycle of vibrational codependency. I felt everyone else's experience and couldn't relax in my body until everyone around me was more at ease. It was an exhausting way to live, and yet, I seemed to be a kid on a mission. For some reason, it felt more important to help others feel better and contemplate the mysteries of the Universe than anything else the world had to offer.

While I was raised in a very loving family and had a wonderful childhood in many respects, I was very much an adult in a child's body. The frenetic energy of other children was often too much for me to handle. I always preferred a playground when I was the only child there. As soon as a band of wild kids invaded the swing set, it was my cue to leave. Looking back, I was frightened by the energy I felt within them and intimidated by how rough they played. My kind of fun was much more passive. I loved dancing in the joy of imagination and talking with adults.

Anytime adults spoke about the deeper aspects of life, I felt the energy in the room shift into a more expansive state. I didn't know what was happening, but I liked how it felt. This attracted me to anything that caused such a shift to occur.

It seemed as if the expansion of energy allowed me to feel relaxed in a way that was so often missing from my life.

Whenever I was able to feel this profound depth of relaxation, I was no longer so overwhelmed with other people's feelings or in need of making anyone feel better.

An Empathic Misunderstanding

These spontaneous expansions of energy became the first of many unexplainable mystical experiences that I encountered. Like so many naturally intuitive children, I was open and receptive to the higher realms of the Universe, without knowing them to be anything other than "how life is." Once I began talking about my experiences, I was amazed to learn how unique they were. This confused and astounded me to no end. How was it possible that everyone else wasn't able to feel and see what I was feeling and seeing so clearly?

I share this with you because perhaps you too are empathic and on a similar journey. It can be painful, overwhelming, and confusing not to know how to make your way through a world where you might be inundated by the emotional heaviness of others and distracted by the patterns that other people are resolving within themselves.

As empathic beings, we often feel the emotional barriers in the hearts of our friends and family members but misunderstand it as proof of a lack of love toward us. This can lead to feeling as if we must not be worthy enough for love. It can also lead to believing that maybe we haven't worked hard enough to earn their approval. Of course what we are innocently doing is blaming ourselves for other people's experiences.

In many instances, all we know is *I don't feel what I wish to feel, and I'm going to do everything in my power to free the people around me of their burdens so there's nothing in the way of them loving me the way I want to be loved.*

When we feel affected by other people's burdens or limited by what others can't provide us, this can serve as a reminder that we deserve more love, not less.

Entering the Garden

While vibrational codependency inundated my life, there were recurring mystical experiences that quickly turned my childhood into a mystery that I was determined to solve. I remember being around a group of adults when I happened to say something that stunned everyone into silence. While they seemed amazed by the wisdom that seemed to effortlessly flow out of me, I had no idea what I was saying. When I was asked how I knew what I had said, my response was, "It's like whispering into my own self's ear." While the group of adults marveled at my seven-year-old response, I had absolutely no idea why they were so astounded, nor did I even know the meaning of the words that I spoke. This became the first of many instances in which I would say things that amazed others without having a single clue as to what I was talking about. Like many naturally intuitive children, I wasn't mature enough to understand the human condition or to acknowledge the depth of insight that came forth from my young self.

During that time, I was mostly attracted to any subject matter that created an energetic shift. I remember stumbling upon books on UFOs and ESP. When the energy within me began to shift just by scanning each page, I was instantly fascinated with every subject of paranormal phenomenon. For some unexplainable reason, the idea of moving objects with your mind, flying, or even time travel seemed oddly familiar to me. While many kids were interested in becoming star athletes on the football field or basketball court, I was like a different type of athlete in training. My sport was tapping into the unlimited power of the mind.

I remember being so fascinated with the mystery of psychic superpowers. It wasn't as if I was determined to prove any of those abilities were real. I already knew in my heart how real they were and just felt soothed by the expansion of energy that I felt when I experienced them.

If anything, the doubt and skepticism many people had toward these topics made me feel like I was living on the wrong planet.

Some of my more pivotal mystical experiences occurred when I was ten years old. I remember a little brick wall dividing my friend's house from his neighbor's property. When I walked by the wall, something caught my attention and stopped me mid-step. I just stared at the wall. In my mind, I heard a voice say, "I am not the wall. I am not this body. I am the space between it." At such a young age, I had no idea what any of this meant. I felt as if I would know its meaning sometime in the future, but at the time, I didn't have the maturity or awareness to acknowledge the wisdom that had been given to me.

Shortly after that insight, one of my most life-changing experiences occurred in what I thought was a dream. As it began, I immediately found myself in the most beautiful garden I had ever seen. The colors were so vivid. It was as if various hues of light were pouring out in every direction. It was absolutely surreal and the most loved I had ever felt, especially since love wasn't an emotion I distinctly remember in my earlier years.

I knew the relief of peace that came whenever energy expanded, but I never really felt love or even noticed a lack of it. From as far back as I can remember, the predominant feeling I experienced most often was vastness. It felt like an emptiness that was neither full nor lacking anything at all. But now, as I looked around the garden, I instantly felt at home and was filled with an undeniable sense of feeling safe and held.

In front of me, I could see a field of waist-high flowers. As I began moving through the thick grasses, I suddenly realized I was also simultaneously hovering above them. I didn't know how I was having two experiences at once or even how I was able to float above things. It didn't seem to matter since the intensity of love held me in such a magnificently gentle way. As I floated toward the middle of the field, I noticed an illuminated being hovering above them as well. He was about twenty feet in front of me. From my vantage point, he appeared to be a man with dark hair and a beard wearing a white robe that covered his feet. For some reason, he felt very familiar and wise to me. He motioned me toward him, and I just froze.

Moments later, I began spontaneously floating in his direction. As I got nearly five feet from him, I could see his eyes, but I couldn't see any pupils. It was as though a river of white light poured out of his eyes. This reminded me of scary movies I had seen in which people roll their eyes up into their head. *Why was I thinking of such a thing during this experience?* Just having that thought interrupted the flow of the moment. I remember falling through the field of flowers, which then led to falling through the sky until I crashed back into my body. It was only when I landed back in my body that I realized I had left it.

My breathing was heavy, and I was freezing cold while dripping with sweat. As I attempted to process this experience, I noticed the same man who had hovered above the field of flowers. This time he was standing in my doorway as an outline of chalky white energy. Out of the corner of my eye, I saw this being motion me toward him once again. As I looked directly at him, he suddenly disappeared.

This experience left me with more questions than answers. Even so, the feeling of love from the garden was so immense that it remains just as strong and noticeable at the core of my being after all these years.

I remember talking with my parents about this experience the day after it occurred, and I noticed their interest deepening with every vivid detail. Once I finished, my father recalled a story in which he had nearly the same experience during an afternoon meditation approximately thirty years earlier. He remembered leaving his body, entering a garden, hovering above a beautiful field of flowers, and encountering a being in a white robe, just as I had.

This helped me acknowledge a profound sense of interconnection at play that doesn't need to be understood in order to be explored. From this point forward, I was filled with an all-encompassing sense of awe and wonder, as the love I felt in the garden seemed to guide my every breath.

Guided by Love

Later that day, another incredible experience occurred as I walked to a friend's house. All of a sudden, I noticed in my peripheral vision more illuminated beings outlined in white chalky energy walking on both sides of me. As I saw this, an instinct told me they were spirit guides, who would escort me through every stage of my life. For some reason, it wasn't strange or exciting, just oddly familiar. I knew they were safe and trustworthy since they emanated the same vibration of love I remember feeling in the garden. That became the first time I had a vividly deep knowing without understanding how I suddenly knew it. As I entered my friend's house, I saw a framed painting hanging on the wall of his living room. I remember saying, "I know him!"

My friend responded, "Yeah, Matt. We all know him. That's Jesus."

"I met him last night," I said with absolute certainty. My friend just glared at me. "C'mon! You didn't meet Jesus."

I remember feeling such an irrefutable knowing that I *had* met Jesus while not understanding why meeting him seemed so inappropriate or unfathomable. Had I broken a cardinal rule in the Universe? Did this mean I couldn't celebrate Hanukkah anymore?

Despite those questions, there was a palpable knowing that many answers would be revealed in the upcoming chapters of my life. All I had to do was stay tuned as the guides lovingly escorted me with every step. It wasn't as if they were there to give me every answer. Instead, they eased my uncertainties by helping me notice a flow of perfection that was woven throughout all experiences—no matter the outcome they produced. That allowed me to embrace each moment on an existential level while playing the role of a character who often seemed anything but okay with the circumstances at hand.

After a while, I forgot the guides were even there, as the majority of my attention was consumed by adolescence. Very shortly after my eighteenth birthday, the guides began speaking to me. I remember the first time it happened. It was like a booming voice emanating from within the center of my body. I wasn't frightened because it carried the vibration of love I remembered experiencing in the garden so many years before. The first thing I heard was a voice saying, "You're not who you think you are." For some reason, "Who the heck are you?" was my immediate response.

From that point forward, I began daily dialogues with my spirit guides while sitting in my bedroom. They introduced themselves as Ascended Masters and Archangels. Each one came with a distinct color to symbolize their vibrational frequency as well as mental pictures to confirm whom I was speaking with.

As unique as each Archangel and Ascended Master seemed to be, they all transmitted such loving energy. This made it safe for me to openly engage. I also began to notice these dialogues were helping to attune my intuitive abilities into a heightened state of refinement. It was as if these conversations were assisting me in elevating my antenna and adjusting the dial to receive the clearest signal.

Whenever I spoke to an Archangel or an Ascended Master, I received a symbolic vision of their message. At the same time, I heard their insights as clearly as if I was speaking to someone on the phone. While that occurred, I also felt sensations in my body that provided information, much like how a computer downloads new files. This helped me understand that I had the intuitive abilities of seeing, hearing, and feeling, which seemed to work together in a harmonious sense of spontaneous knowing.

I had a sense that I was being prepared for something, but I didn't know what. The answer wasn't immediately obvious, but it began revealing itself in the most random of places. Out of nowhere, I would receive a sudden download of information and be guided to walk up to someone I'd never met and deliver a message. Every time it happened, I was so afraid of being judged or rejected, along with a fear of offering a message they may not understand.

I remember thinking, *What if I'm just crazy, and I don't even know it?* Thankfully, I never hesitated to deliver a message since the inspiration was so strong. I felt as though I was about to have a heart attack if I didn't share the message with them. That helped me get over a fear of rejection as well as my belief in self-doubt. Each time it became easier to do so, as every message provided powerful moments of transformation.

From my perspective, it was like stepping up to the plate with a bat in your hand and not knowing what to do with it. Then, all of sudden, a ball is tossed your way. Before you can even think, your body swings the bat and hits the ball out of the park. While everyone cheers your accomplishment, you remain baffled at the fact that this seems to work perfectly each time, even without knowing how it works or what you're even doing to make it happen.

From there, I was guided into spiritual bookstores to deliver more spontaneous messages. I remember catching the eye of the store owner who asked me if I could offer intuitive readings. The feeling in my body answered with a resounding "Yes," so apparently, this is what I was supposed to do. People sat down with me and for half a second, I'd have absolutely no idea what to do. Then, like clockwork, it all began to flow.

While delivering each message freed me from feeling as though I was about to have a heart attack, I still had no idea what was going on. Since it felt so good to be in the flow of energy and everyone got so much out of it, I just went along for the ride.

Within two months, I was a featured reader at psychic fairs with a regular schedule of clients. To my amazement, the majority of people who wanted my help were other readers and healers. It was as if they couldn't figure out how I channeled messages in such a clear and compelling way. While everyone else seemed astounded, I was terrified most of the time. I was just following the guidance I received and allowing the feeling of love to carry me along.

Initially, I was delivering messages to individuals, but it quickly expanded into teachings that I offered to groups. It was as if any assembly of people created a group soul where I was intuitively guided to offer teachings that resonated in the lives of everyone in attendance. At that point, I was starting to get more comfortable in that role. I was trusting in the fact that something I could not explain was happening on a regular basis to uplift the lives of everyone I encountered.

Exploring the Akashic Records

It was during this moment of acceptance that I was called into a meeting with the Archangels and Ascended Masters. They had something wonderfully important to share that produced a feeling of excitement in my body. I was asked to close my eyes, and as I did, my consciousness was immediately whisked off into a different location. As soon as I arrived, what I saw looked like the Lincoln Memorial with huge white pillars.

An intuition told me I had arrived at the Akashic Records. From my perspective, it appeared to be a huge library. I was told that every book I saw contained the soul contracts of each lifetime and every personal encounter. Once the wisdom occupied in each contract was understood and fully absorbed by that individual, the Ascended Master or Archangel assigned to their soul's journey cleared the contract out of that person's book. This process seemed like a recurring graduation ceremony that constantly welcomed brand-new chapters of growth and expansion into one's life.

While I received this instant download of information, I walked to the top of the stairs toward a glowing light table adjacent to the entrance. The Ascended Masters and Archangels were standing there rejoicing in my arrival. I remember thinking how surreal it all was. As they stood in front of me, beaming with admiration, it gave me the impression I was about to graduate to a new level. That was true, but I had no idea the level of revelation they were about to show me.

Almost on cue, they reached under their chins and lifted up their faces as if they were wearing masks at a masquerade party. Underneath each mask was a reflection of *me*. I remember gasping as I saw this. "They are all me!" But, even as I saw myself underneath each mask, something wasn't clicking into place.

I immediately said, "I don't get it."

We Are You—Awakening the Master Within

My main guide, Melchizedek, filled me in with the following response: "We are not only what you are becoming; we are what you've already become. We are agents of the divine, who have stepped back in time to visit ourselves in spiritual childhood."

When I heard those words, a lifelong heaviness I never knew I was carrying lifted off my shoulders. It also helped me see each person, no matter how kind-hearted or emotionally damaged they seemed to be, as seeds of divinity growing into their true masterful potential. From that point forward, I knew my intuitive gifts would be used to serve the highest destiny of the Universe by awakening the Master in every heart.

This is why I honor our timeless meeting and remain delighted to share these powerful insights in celebration of the Master who awakens in you. Whether you know it or not, the mystery of your own existence has been inviting you inward since the dawn of creation. With love as your guide, now is the time to answer the call.

No matter the details or circumstances consuming your attention, the light of your highest potential can now be revealed.

Four Simple Words

Despite all of these experiences, it is my belief that my spiritual journey did not truly begin until I was in my midtwenties. Prior to then, I was a very empathic child with pronounced intuitive abilities, having many vivid experiences of awakening that many people to this day continue to chase and pursue. Yet, in my midtwenties I had a very clear realization. I realized that no matter how many mystical experiences I had, no matter how deeply I could feel into the people around me, or how clearly I could transmit messages that positively affected so many lives, those were not actual benchmarks for my spiritual evolution. I began to see that despite my abilities, I was still very much fighting and negotiating with life in the same way those who hadn't had any of those experiences were.

It helped me to put into perspective that while I was having those transcendent experiences, I knew in my heart that I could not define myself by them in any way. Instead, I needed to establish a new spiritual benchmark for myself. I quickly began to see how often I would fight or negotiate with life as a sign of how infrequently I trusted in the faith of the divine plan. While I continued to share the intuitively guided messages that came to me in front of larger groups, something even deeper was blossoming within me.

During that time, I remember talking to the Universe and saying, "May I be a conduit of awakened consciousness. May I heal what is unresolved in every heart, and may I bring forth what will finally satisfy my desire to be the One I already am."

Within a few days, a response came during a dialogue I had with the Universe, in the form of four simple words: "Whatever arises, love that."

Based on my open line of communication with my spirit guides, I could have very well asked for some clarification. On the other hand, what's so interesting is that even though I could have called upon their guidance in any given moment, the most extraordinary experience often was to feel my way into it. It's kind of like forgetting the end of a movie you've already watched just so you can experience it again for the very first time.

I didn't really want to know what was meant by those four words; I just wanted to test it out, to see what would be revealed. So I took these words literally: *Okay, Universe—whatever arises, love that.* On a walk around my neighborhood, I saw a flock of birds fly by and I thought, *Well, that got my attention; that's arising,* so I said, "I love you." Part of me didn't know if that was right, but I just followed the impulse since I felt the love of the garden inspiring me to move in that direction.

I continued walking around my neighborhood and saw a city worker who was using a jackhammer at a construction site. It startled me, and I thought, *Well, that's arising. Love that!* And so I sent an "I love you" silently to the city worker in view.

I continued to send love to anything that got my attention. As I did this, I began to see every person, place, and thing as works of art on exhibit in the museum of divinity, where I was both a visitor as well as a work of art on display. The more love I sent to whatever captured my attention, the more I felt the love of the garden coming alive in me. As love was offered, the more I recognized who I really am—an innocent expression of divine will and not a person in search of it.

By following the instructions of those four simple words, I realized myself to be life's eternal liberator, instead of a person waiting to be liberated from the pitfalls of life. I quickly began to see that everything in life was orchestrated by the highest intelligence of the Universe. From one moment to the next, it only brought forward the experiences that triggered emotions that had never been loved by anyone else. As I would love these feelings in my body, I could also intuitively sense that I was embracing the feelings that were unresolved in all bodies.

I began to see that as I healed myself, I was transforming the fabric of reality for the well-being of all.

Despite having many life-changing awakening experiences, that practice was the most fulfilling of all. It even satisfied the constant hunger of my deepest spiritual desires. The more I loved whatever captured my attention, the more vivid of an awakening was revealed. I remember when this occurred during another walk in my neighborhood. It was as if I walked around my block and the one who started the walk never returned.

While my body made a loop around the neighborhood, the one who thought he was taking each step simply didn't come back. I was aware of breathing, moving, and feeling, but there was no sense of self defined by it. There were just experiences arising within a spaciousness brimming with the feeling of being back in the garden. There wasn't even a sense of this being an amazing experience since there wasn't anyone it described—good, bad, or otherwise. The one thing I remember when this happened was that it felt like the Earth stopped moving or as if time suddenly vanished. The most surprising part of all was how comfortable this felt without my knowing why or even having a need to question, contemplate, or understand.

Shortly after this experience, I heard what I thought was an explosion. While investigating to see if I was hearing the sound of gunshots, I realized that the sounds turned out to be something exploding in my own head. I wasn't afraid or panicked, just naturally open. As the explosion occurred, it felt as if my entire sense of self was oozing out of my ears like warm liquid light.

From that point forward, I no longer had any sense of who I was as a person. Even deeper than the experience I had walking around my neighborhood, it was as if all reference points of who I am and what I'm not completely ceased to exist. And yet, there was an "I" that remained—an infinite "I" that was nothing but radiance masquerading in form. This "I" was here to bring forth the divinity of others, as a way for the Universe to consciously play in the ecstasy of its own immaculate presence.

As magnificent of a realization as that seemed to be, it didn't feel as if my consciousness was done expanding in any way. If anything, those experiences accelerated in frequency, with no foreseeable end to what was being revealed. At that point in my journey, I didn't know those experiences were merely the beginning of an even greater recognition of truth that would occur a few years later. As it unfolded, it honored everything I had ever learned by showing me a depth of clarity that made everything I knew completely obsolete.

That wasn't done to destroy my treasured insights. Instead, it assisted me into a brand-new level of consciousness where I wasn't bound by any degree of knowing or burdened by the wisdom I had previously learned.

To make matters even more surreal, a profound awakening, even greater than the ones I've just shared, occurred while I was eating dinner at a restaurant. All of a sudden, everything began to change. The sound of voices from the patrons sitting at other tables started to echo in my ears. It was as if they were all expressions of my own consciousness while appearing around me as a play of different characters.

I began looking around at the people at nearby tables and noticed every physical trait and emotional quality seemed oddly embellished. It was as if everyone was molded out of this strange energetic clay. I remember looking at everyone around me and having the thought, *They are trying so hard to stay in character, but this isn't who they are at all.* It was as if their human identity had become a façade where everyone was working diligently to maintain some sort of personal image.

At that point, the server presented me with the fish tacos I forgot I had ordered. As I looked at the plate, I saw particles of vibrating energy that gave the appearance of a solid plate of food. I also witnessed these same particles in the table, throughout my body, and within everyone at the restaurant. Soon, the vibrating particles appeared to be a formless blanket of energy with everything somehow appearing within an all-encompassing misty energy field.

I began to laugh at the simultaneous nature of my experience. Here I was eating a plate of fish tacos, while on an energetic level, nothing was happening at all. Couples could laugh, babies would cry, servers could drop entire trays of food, and nothing disturbed the field of energy. I began to see every person as a creative way in which energy was expressing itself—from the mundane to the outrageous. Because I was seeing this from an energetic position, I realized my "self" to *be* the entire field of energy. As this field, each person, place, and thing celebrated my own infinite potential in physical form.

It wasn't a sense of *I am doing this from a belief in personal control. It was a direct realization of "I" as the eternal One in all.* As perfectly timed as could be, the server approached my table and asked how my fish tacos were. I remember laughing and saying, "Beyond belief." She smiled and scurried off to the next table as I sat back and marveled at the cosmic irony of life.

Imagine: she's having her experience of a satisfied customer while I'm watching the entire Universe come alive in a restaurant where others are eating and conversing among themselves. At that point, I realized how we are each living in our own worlds, while interacting within the same eternal space. It was at that defining moment that I acknowledged the two-fold realization of truth. *We are One in our essence but remain different as individuals.* Between these two extremes, your journey is revealed.

Just as I had reached such a defining moment of clarity, the experience continued to open up way beyond anything I had ever known or could ever imagine. As it occurred, I received an intuition instructing me to go home and rest. I sensed that I would be spending the evening integrating this powerful realization on an energetic level.

I remember walking to the car and feeling the gravitational pull of the Earth's orbit so strongly I had to hold onto other cars as I made my way through the parking lot. As soon as I got home, I wrapped myself in a blanket and called it a day. I intuitively knew my life would never be the same, so I just allowed the Universe to do what needed to be done.

At that point, everything dissolved into emptiness. I no longer existed in a world of any kind. I was nothing. As nothing, I felt intermittent waves of ecstasy and terror. As I explored those sensations, I realized I wasn't actually in ecstasy or terror at all. It was the memory of how life used to be compared to how things were right in that moment that caused those waves of conflicting emotion to erupt.

I then realized that sensations of emptiness only seemed like nothing when compared to memories of something else.

As I understood this, both ideas of emptiness and something in form equally dropped away.

There was nothing but emptiness with no one to claim or deny it in any way. It was an absolute void space—absent of location, description, quality, or distinction. There was no fear, no loss, no grief, no pain, no pressure, or any idea whatsoever.

I instantly realized, *I am a void of nothing that is void of nothing.*

To my amazement, what remained was the most intimate sense of self that had been here all along. Instead of being a person with a lingering remembrance of visiting the garden at a young age, *I was the garden of divinity itself. While "decorated" as a person living in a world, in truth, I am an eternal space through which all things come to life.* I remember seeing so obviously how the void, which is the Source of all things, witnesses everything by *being* it all.

I thought, *Maybe if I just hang out here, I'll be whisked away into another character or adventure.* As I waited, nothing happened. Then waiting disappeared, along with every idea I had ever imagined. Soon everything faded to black just like a character dying in a movie.

I didn't exactly know what was happening, but I had a sense that death had come. It was here for me, and I was ready to make it easy for death to do whatever it does. For some reason, I had never felt more comforted. I was completely aware of myself without reference points or limitations of any kind.

Even though it felt like a brand-new beginning, I couldn't help but feel like something within me had come to an end. As I drew in what might've been the final breath I'd ever take, I surrendered to death once and for all.

At that moment, my final thought was *Lord, take me—I'm yours.* It was at that moment that my ego was laid to rest once and for all.

As I lay there surrendering myself to death, nothing else happened. The void of nothing that is void of nothing remained while the body relaxed into sleep. As the void, I watched the body sleep from within the body. I noticed I was aware of sleeping, but I was not asleep at all. I was an ever-present aliveness aware of however the body seemed to be.

The next morning, I woke up wondering if everything that had transpired the night before was some sort of dream, but as it turned out, the experience of being the void was just as prominent as the night before. With no other alternative, I closed my eyes and gazed into the emptiness of existence.

I thought, *Maybe this is it. Maybe I'll just spend an eternity in this all-consuming space.* Nearly right on cue, out of the silent depths of an eternal void emerged a spontaneous desire to know one's self. As this desire blossomed, a beam of energy emanated out of nowhere and transformed the void space into an endless field of light. Within the light, every person, place, and thing sprouted into form. It was here to play out, in endless dimensions of time and space, every characteristic, situation, and outcome in existence.

I was the void, the desire to know itself, the field of light birthed out of it, and everything within it all at once. As I gazed into the beauty of form, I saw the light within each person, place, and thing like a sunray expressing the radiance of its Source. At that point, I was intuitively told, "The light of all is the soul of One. The soul of One is the One I AM."

I was both the nothing through which everything came into existence, everything appearing in its earthly form, as well as the love that embraced it all.

This life-changing recognition also brought forth an intuitive knowing of "resurrection" as an essential stage of growth throughout every journey. This helped me understand death as a doorway into the paradise of resurrection where nothing but love remains.

For many who inhabit this planet, the willingness to enter the doorway of death and be reborn as the light of love in form remains a central theme in the journey of awakening. Whether you are a grocery store checker, a stay-at-home mom, an executive, or even a lifelong spiritual seeker, we have arrived at an exciting chapter of human evolution where consciousness is awakening without the body needing to dissolve. With love as your guide, every stage of your journey, including the dissolving of ego and the resurrection of the soul, can unfold with clarity, compassion, peace, and ease.

Your Heart as the Center of the Universe

With love leading the way, your heart can be seen as the center of the Universe. From this space of recognition, you may realize: through the heart that you embrace, all things are transformed.

Whether you stop in moments of turmoil to support your innocence through unexpected change or in the aftermath of devastating loss, you always have the power to expand your consciousness, simply by taking the time to honor yourself more often. Even when everything seems fine in your life, you can always stop throughout your day, knowing the love that you cultivate is always sent to all hearts in existence.

While you may appear to be one person loving one heart, the blessings and resources that you offer are infinite and far-reaching. It's never a matter of anyone being excluded when loving your heart is your focus. Since the love you send to the world passes through your heart first, you are the first one your blessings touch as they ripple out to every soul.

You can think of your heart as a shipping dock for the endless blessings of divinity, where all wishes, dreams, and desires are sent out to be granted in the lives of every dreamer.

Imagine the miraculous implications you cultivate by loving your heart more often. Perhaps a farmer who depends on growing crops to feed his family discovers a greater harvest than ever before. As a result, maybe they are able to afford gifts for their family during the holiday season. What if someone who was stuck in an abusive relationship spontaneously finds the courage to move into an environment that honors their true worth and value? What if such courage came to these people as a result of *your* loving choices?

Perhaps a country inundated by drought, unable to grow crops to feed their communities, all of a sudden finds changes in weather that fertilize the soil of their land. As they spontaneously rejoice in the miracle that allows them to grow food and nourish so many families, they may not even know this was made possible by a momentum of energy created by you loving your own heart.

This doesn't mean that you are ever the cause of anything you see. More precisely, you are the solution emerging in every form. Even if you misunderstand these words and feel guilty about not loving yourself enough to support the well-being of all, it becomes another opportunity to embrace your guilt as the next one in line to be loved. As you welcome guilt with open arms, you are assisting in releasing it out of the collective unconsciousness for the well-being of all.

Although loving what arises can help you to immediately transform discomfort into something more preferable and spacious, I encourage you to take this practice beyond the benefits of a conventional healing modality. Instead of using this practice as a cosmic fire extinguisher to merely resolve the flames of personal despair, I invite you to treasure your heart on a regular basis, until the world you are viewing reflects back the light that your love reveals.

The Heart of Surrender

IT IS COMMON for seekers to anticipate spiritual evolution as a static event or one gigantic moment of realization. Throughout my journey, though, I have come to see how your deepest discoveries are not typically contained in a specific mystical event, but are rather a lifetime of realizations that increase over time. As the maturity of your path unfolds, it becomes easier to see how you cannot define the progression of your journey by how many mystical experiences or awakenings you've had since many more are sure to come. Equally so, there is no need to judge yourself, as if you are falling behind by not having the experiences that others seem to encounter. While moments of transcendence are incredible to behold, the true benchmark of spiritual maturity is how often your words and actions are aligned with love.

The willingness to allow your choices to come from a place of love no matter the outcomes or circumstances at hand is what I call *the heart of surrender.* This shift into heart-centered consciousness makes welcoming each moment with openness, kindness, and compassion more vital than what you hope to gain from life. Instead of trying to control the things you can't seem to change, you redefine the way you relate to the world.

The heart of surrender is accessed by asking a bold series of questions. They are not questions that require you to search for an answer but to unearth a visceral response in your body to confirm your deepest wisdom. To enter the heart of surrender, I invite you to ask yourself the following questions:

> What happens if I stop fighting the things that
> seem to fight with me? What happens if instead
> of trying to change the behavior of others, I
> become the first one to stop fighting, even if
> others still fight with me?

What do you feel in your body when asking these questions? Even if there is a sensation of fear, the mere consideration of no longer fighting against the things that fight with you becomes another opportunity to release unconscious patterns just by loving the heart that feels so threatened.

Perhaps your innocence believes that to stop fighting would result in being overpowered, hurt, or feeling unsafe. What if the circumstances of your life are not what are making you feel unsafe? What if it's your willingness to fight that causes you to feel so disempowered? Without a need to blame anyone for your experiences, what then happens to the sensation of fear?

If you can sense a willingness to fight within you, this is surely the next one in line to be on the receiving end of your loving attention. Perhaps you've never loved the part of you that fights because you've been busy joining its crusade. Maybe you've pushed that part of yourself to the background when it didn't seem to act in a spiritually appropriate manner. Whether agreeing with the reasons that justify a fight or trying to get your most relentless thoughts to change their position, within these two extremes, the one who needs something to fight or fix has never been loved as an equal expression of divinity. To resolve this oversight, please repeat the following healing mantra:

> I accept that the aspect of self that fights is only here to be loved as only I can love it. I acknowledge that the aspect of self that fights is not in a fight with anything or anyone but is actually fighting for the beauty, ecstasy, and perfection of my own loving attention.

> I accept that the aspect of self that fights—that is fueled by a need to be right or have the final word—is only fighting for my attention.

> Since this innocence is only fighting for my attention, I no longer fight against the things that I think are fighting with me. Instead, I offer loving-kindness to the innocence that no longer has to work so hard to receive my support.

In repeating these words, can you feel a struggle coming to an end that doesn't leave you immersed in doubt or shrouded in fear? Maybe there is a realization that while it feels as if there's much to fight, defend, fix, change, or even maintain, there is an innocence within you that uses these tendencies as attention-seeking devices.

Just by recognizing how often you act out the very behavior that cries for your own heart-centered support, you have boldly taken another step forward in an exciting new direction.

Creating Your Own Personal Love Statement

The next step in the heart of surrender is creating your own personal love statement. Although you can find much benefit from embracing your heart one "I love you" at a time, such an offering is just the beginning. A personal love statement is very powerful especially if the words "I love you" come with memories you would prefer to bury. It is very possible that you've heard encouraging words from those who wanted to love you but wound up lashing out in moments of frustration, anger, and desperation. If that is the case, there may be painful associations in your subconscious mind that obscure your view of love based on the actions of those who hurt you the most.

Creating your personal love statement begins by asking yourself the following questions:

> What are the words I never heard that I always
> wanted to hear? Who in my experience hurt me
> the most? And what are the words they never
> said that really would have allowed my healing
> to occur?

Whatever words arise are always valid, since any information you receive could only be the authority of your highest wisdom.

Sometimes with unresolved pain, you do not need someone from your past to say "I love you" if they were never able to do so. Instead, you might need them to say "I'm sorry. I was wrong." Your personal love statement can evolve day-by-day, week-by-week, and sometimes even minute-by-minute. Whatever you never heard from someone else or wanted to hear more often becomes the words you offer yourself.

Just as you may have practiced with "I love you," you can respond to any emotional upheaval by repeating your personal love statement in two-minute intervals as many times a day as you need. Even when you're not caught in storms of personal turmoil, you can continue offering your personal love statement as a way of uplifting and blessing all beings in existence.

As your personal love statement is created or modified, it's important to allow your innocence to fully participate in the process. In order to dissolve each threat and end your fight with life, it is crucial to uncover the words you've always wanted to hear. Maybe they are the words that you have heard but not often enough, or maybe these words were never spoken in an authentic tone of voice.

What if the words you've always wanted to hear can be inspired from a spiritual or even a religious context? If so, what are the words your Source could say that would make you feel as if you can do no wrong? What could be said that allows you to fully be yourself? What would you need to hear to unlock your potential and bring it forward for the liberation of all?

As you may already be starting to see, your personal love statement establishes a deeper level of communication with your heart. Even if you were shunned, silenced, or overpowered in the past, your inner child is always willing to be a part of your healing journey. When you offer your personal love statement with patience, softness, and consistency, your heart will soon open up and share with you the secrets that ensure your growth and expansion.

As a way of discovering the words you've always wanted to hear or never heard often enough, please repeat the following phrases:

> You matter.
> You are enough.
> You are worthy of being seen and heard.
> You are special.
> There is a reason you are here.
> You are beautiful.
> You are so talented.
> I always want to know how you feel.
> Please don't hold back.
> You are perfect just the way you are.
> I am so blessed and honored to have you in my life.
> Thank you for forgiving me.
> I am so sorry for all that I have done to you.
> I did not know how deeply you were hurt.
> I'm sorry I did not consider your feelings.
> I was wrong.
> You don't have to forgive me if you don't want to.
> Your talent knows no limits.

Perhaps one or more of these phrases satisfies a heartfelt desire to hear the words that seemed missing from your past. If so, can you become the one who offers your heart the gifts it has waited to receive for far too long?

No matter how you wish to be treated by others, can you be the one who supports your emotional needs with greater consistency and enthusiasm than ever before?

The Difference between Victimhood and Empowerment

In the heart of surrender, the difference between victimhood and empowerment is simple; in victimhood you hold yourself emotionally hostage while waiting for others to tell you what they may not be able to say. Until they do, you remain at odds with life, blaming those who haven't spoken the words you need to hear as the reason for your suffering. As this occurs, you are more likely to defend yourself at every turn and fight against the things that no amount of effort ever seems to change.

On the other hand, empowerment is not about waiting for other people to say the right words at all. It is realizing how you are the one who needs to say the things that you've waited your entire life to hear. No matter how much you wish to be validated by others, only the one who survived each ordeal could ever be the one to speak the words your past seemed to withhold. As the one who endured each struggle and overcame every obstacle, only you hold the key to opening your heart by supporting yourself in a more consistent and intimate way.

Since your subconscious mind does not know the difference between someone else saying certain words and you saying them to yourself, your heart will heal the same way even if the words don't come from the person of your choosing.

With each step forward, the heart of surrender frees you from viewing your life through the eyes of victimhood. Instead of seeing all the people who lash out, verbally assault, judge, or criticize, you can recognize such behavior as desperate ways their innocence cries out for the attention they don't know how to give to themselves. In recognizing this deeper truth, you can give their heart the loving attention that no one else may have ever provided by offering a more gracious response than their actions deserve. Even if you cannot dare to love the heart of another in response to their cruelty, you can always remove yourself from volatile situations and allow your own heart to become your point of focus. As your heart is honored, blessings are sent to everything in existence, including the ones who lash out, without you having to do anything else but acknowledge the innocence within you who feels mistreated.

In the heart of surrender, treating people far better than they treat you becomes an acceptable way to live, especially because their inability to treat you well has nothing to do with you, but reflects the kind of relationship they have with themselves. This allows you to forget how to be a victim when the unconscious actions of another clearly reveal a heart in need of healing and a child lost in pain. Whether someone glares at you while drowning in their own self-judgment or you find yourself hurt by someone you deeply admire, you have every right to accept a more noble invitation to love yourself more, not less.

To take your next step in the heart of surrender, please repeat this healing mantra:

I no longer fight with those who insist on fighting with me. I acknowledge anyone who fights as only fighting for the grace of their own loving attention.

I freely give loving attention to whatever calls out for it, whether appearing as jumbled emotions in my body, a noisy mind of endless thoughts, or the relentless behavior of those I encounter.

By speaking to others in a tone and manner that suggests how much better they deserve to treat themselves when not in my presence, I help raise the vibration of the planet. I know full well that my path cannot be defined by how others treat me but only how I choose to respond.

Even though it seems as if I'm speaking to other characters in my play, as the truth of all that is, whatever I say to another is a love letter sent to every heart. Knowing this, I relinquish any desire or tendency to fight, negotiate, or defend, and I return to love by embracing the truth of all.

Whether or not those I love consciously receive my gifts, it is I who walks away from each encounter more open, conscious, and empowered than any moment before.

Choices and Outcomes

In the heart of surrender, you are no longer matching other people's behavior with the same frequency of unconsciousness. Because you have greater respect toward yourself, you are able to recognize the cruelty of others as coming from those who are entrenched in too much personal turmoil to remember their divinity, let alone consider your feelings with the respect they deserve.

Personal turmoil is often a sign that a person is totally engulfed in a healing crisis they may not even know is happening. Those who are embroiled in drama but completely unaware of the spiritual opportunities presented in every breath can be viewed as innocent beings who just don't know anything deeper than the surface of life. Whether you believe others deserve your kindness or not, their situation can always become another opportunity to say to yourself the words you would love to hear from them. This transforms any identity of victimhood into the embodied grace of love in action, so you no longer hold yourself emotionally hostage awaiting someone else's attention, respect, or validation as your ransom.

One moment of surrender at a time, you become more aware of what you need to provide for yourself rather than spending your time arguing with those who are fueled by fighting. On an even more intimate level, you also begin to realize something important about the power of choice. Instead of imagining how choices are ways to control outcomes or manipulate reality, you see each choice from a higher perspective.

Each of your choices correlates to a vibrational frequency. While it isn't necessary to understand the exact frequency as a number, it's important to use your emotional body as an energetic barometer. Choices aligned with a high vibration often bring excitement, ease, and relaxation into your body. The choices reflecting a low vibration feel contracted, heavy, and fill you with doubt, shame, guilt, worry, or resentment.

Many of us have been conditioned to make choices from a fear of missing out on opportunities, which stems from a belief that your choices create outcome. As your consciousness expands, you realize that outcomes are orchestrated by the Universe only to put you into the exact situation to awaken your next highest level of consciousness.

While outcomes cannot be guaranteed, the feeling produced as you tune into each choice provides a sneak preview of what it's going to feel like throughout the duration of any decision. It's as if someone invited you to dinner and you had a feeling of expansion within your heart. This wouldn't ensure that your meal would be delicious; it couldn't guarantee that you would get a reservation at your favorite restaurant or take away from the fact that you might end up waiting an hour for a table to be ready. No matter what the circumstances turned out to be, the feelings you notice when considering choices let you know the type of experience you are capable of having. It's as if your emotions are telling you, "Here is what it's going to feel like by venturing in this direction with no consideration for the circumstances that may come your way."

Since love is the highest vibration in existence, you have the power to bring forth the most incredible experiences by welcoming the decisions that feel most loving to you. When the wisdom of your body reveals which options are aligned with love, your life becomes a more inspired, enjoyable, and fulfilling journey to explore.

Making Decisions from the Heart

What if you were to take a permanent vacation from the intensity of self-doubt by allowing your heart to make each decision? When you allow your body to determine the most relaxed, loving, or exciting choices to make, you no longer have to feel the pressure of wondering what's going to happen or overthink what you should do. By following the feedback of your feelings, your life is guided by a precise flow of intuitive guidance. This frees you from the exhaustion of trying to control a reality that only exists to ensure the fulfillment of your highest destiny.

With intuition leading the way, you also might find yourself naturally expanding the usage of your personal love statement. While it is wonderful to offer yourself the exact words you've always wanted to hear, it becomes even more powerful when you speak such supportive words to those you encounter. Imagine how incredible it would be to offer anyone you meet a compliment or a moment of encouragement, as a way of giving to both hearts the very gift you've always wanted to receive. You might be surprised to realize the words you've been waiting to receive are often the same ones others wish to hear. The fact that you can assist in the healing of another just by speaking out loud the words that mean so much to you reveals an interconnectedness of spirit throughout all time and space.

One inspired choice at a time, there is no longer a fear of making the wrong choice because every decision has been surrendered to the highest authority of love. Whatever arises in the lives of those around you, including yourself, reveals the next moment of healing in the evolution of the whole.

To fully step across the threshold and enter the most exciting stages of spiritual growth, please repeat the following healing mantra:

> I hereby surrender the fate of all of my choices
> to the highest vibration of love. I allow love in
> its purest, most powerful form to fully inhabit
> this body, to speak every word, to choose every
> option, to orchestrate all behaviors, to maneuver
> through each encounter by recognizing each
> moment as a chance to speak to others the very
> words I've always wanted to hear.
>
> I do this, knowing that as I share my personal
> love statement with all I encounter, I am using
> my time on this planet to repeatedly speak out
> loud what I remember not ever receiving from
> the past I so thankfully survived.
>
> From this moment forward, I offer my
> personal love statement as a gift of evolution
> for all. This helps me remember that no matter
> where the finger of blame tends to point, I
> am only crying out for the grace of my own
> loving attention.

Now that I have given love permission to make every choice on my behalf, on some level, I accept that an important stage of my journey is complete.

And so I am free to be the love that I am for the healing, awakening, well-being, and ascension of all. And so it is.

4

Ego, Suffering, and the Overstimulated Nervous System

I REMEMBER WHEN I began to see the importance of love, not just as an instrument of healing, but as a potent transformer of consciousness. It was during a very auspicious conversation I had with my guides, at which time I asked the question, "What is the core of human suffering?"

I asked this question because, in the very beginning of my journey, I became very familiar with the inner workings of ego and came to see it as a central cause of despair. Ego is much like believing you are the character in every scene of a movie, while forgetting that you are really the aliveness within the body of each character acting out various roles. Whether caught up in the storyline of family dynamics, defined by the ups and downs of your work environment, or happy only when those around you are satisfied, an attachment to ego often creates the pain that you hope to resolve. Even though

I could see how much chaos the ego created, there was something inspiring me to look even further.

Perhaps I was drawn to look deeper because there is such a widely accepted spiritual belief that we must develop strategies to transcend ego or try to escape it in some way. While it made sense that so many people would attempt to overcome the very source of their suffering, I didn't feel this was a complete understanding of ego, or even a loving approach. As a result, something motivated me to ask for further clarification.

I asked because I intuitively knew the wisest approach must always be rooted in love. Even when attempting to open the door of liberation or to extinguish the flames of personal despair, a spiritual goal can often become so all-consuming that it becomes easy to go about your journey in a goal-oriented manner.

This reminds me of trick-or-treating as a child on Halloween. My friends and I, dressed in our favorite costumes, were so focused on getting as much free candy and covering as many neighborhoods as possible, we didn't take the time to even give much eye contact or a "thank you" to those who filled our bags. In the same way, you can be so blinded by the number of mystical experiences you collect or how much understanding you hope to find that you may not even take the time to wholeheartedly receive the gifts that have been given to you.

In the heart of surrender, your highest aspiration is to fulfill each goal in the most loving possible way. If there is an imbalance, it will be healed with love. If there is confusion, it will be clarified with love. If there is anything to choose, it will be chosen by love. If there is anything to awaken, it will be awakened by love. This helps you see every precious step on your journey as something beyond a means to an end. It's certainly not about finding the right answer in the back of a textbook or even how well you can articulate what you've learned. Instead, the beauty of your highest wisdom is reflected in how often love influences your decisions.

What Is Ego, Really?

Because the common approach to ego is attempting to control or destroy it in some way, and because love is the missing element in this approach, I knew there had to be something underneath this typical understanding of ego. Whether the goal is turning negative thoughts into more positive ones, silencing the mind, or trying to uncover limiting beliefs with great effort, this approach often leads the most sincere seeker to convert spiritual exploration into a battle for control. Of course, any type of battle can only inflate ego to a more painful degree.

Since love is the highest vibration, everything you encounter—including your worst enemy, your most dramatic experiences, and even the ego itself—must be met with openness, compassion, and care in order to come into contact with the wisest teachings of the Universe. Otherwise, you will find yourself at odds with yourself, discovering new forms of suffering, while attempting to meet your spiritual goals in an overly aggressive manner.

When asking my guides to reveal the core of human suffering, I was initially told, "Ego is a fictitious character that is personified through the roles played in life." From this answer, a few undeniable questions came to mind: I wanted to know why this tendency existed, how to unravel the deepest pains it seemed to cause, and what role it played in the path of awakening.

So I asked my guides, "What is ego, really?" I was told, "Ego is the imaginary identity of an overstimulated nervous system." This answer really struck a chord in me. I wasn't sure what it meant, so I kept asking more questions.

Underneath it all, I came to discover that the source of a closed heart, a noisy mind, low self-esteem, or an out-of-control ego is an *overstimulated nervous system.* If an overstimulated nervous system is the root cause of suffering, the logical question is, how did it become overstimulated?

The primary function of the nervous system is to help maintain a sense of linear order throughout the simultaneous and multidimensional nature of life. Such order is maintained by expelling unknown possibilities orbiting your energy field so you don't have experiences that constantly contradict the integrity of your personal experiences . Until something new has been introduced and accepted by your subconscious mind, it can be overlooked or seem invisible even if it is appearing right in front of you. Just as a group of people can witness the same event and each person sees something that the others may not have seen, each of us views life through a unique lens of perception depending upon how the nervous system maintains order throughout our consciousness. What is known to be true for one person may be invisible or unknown to another. While it appears as if we all inhabit the same planet, everyone lives in their own version of it. The assumption that the world you see is the only one existing is a limiting belief held together by an attachment to ego. As this insistence is confirmed by your perceptions, it creates a tendency to feel dissatisfied or frustrated with life—no matter how justified your ideas seem to be.

When your consciousness is limited through patterns of overstimulation, the nervous system deletes from your perception anything that contradicts your most stringent beliefs. As consciousness expands, engrained beliefs dissolve. In their absence, your nervous system relaxes to welcome the arrival of greater possibilities. These possibilities were there all along but were unrecognizable as long as they were a greater expression of consciousness than you were able to perceive.

One vital reason the nervous system expels potential possibilities out of your view is to assist you in having experiences that you are able to handle. If the blinders suddenly came off, your consciousness would expand so quickly that you'd be disoriented and confused by the multidimensional nature of reality. In many ways, you'd be unable to function in such a state. It would be like living in a hallway of mirrors, not knowing which reflection is yours. While the radiance of your true nature always lives in every form, your nervous system regulates experiences, allowing your consciousness to welcome the arrival of greater possibilities, but in a way that is both natural and ever-revealing.

Even though some have stumbled upon transcendent experiences and had the blinders of unconsciousness suddenly removed, the majority of awakenings are gradual and work in harmony with your nervous system. It is much like a flower enjoying the miracle of blossoming—one petal at a time.

Throughout the history of mysticism, these rare forms of awakenings become spiritual folklore. They can lead many to imagine these dramatic breakthroughs are necessary milestones for the furthering of their journey. When you are captivated by a desire to awaken so quickly, your motivation to explore your spirituality can be tinged with a sense of desperation, insincerity, and overachievement. Ironically, this sense of urgency only serves to overstimulate the nervous system to a greater degree. When this happens, your level of consciousness is constricted to eliminate from view the very experiences being chased.

No matter how many years you have spent immersed in spiritual discourse, the living realization of truth cannot be fully revealed until the nervous system is relaxed. Even on a mystical level, the degree to which a nervous system relaxes also determines who sees angels, ghosts, alternate dimensions, or even receives intuitive messages.

Meanwhile, those entrenched in conditioning may scoff at the possibilities they have yet to see that have always existed around them.

A Psychological Cocoon

Nervous systems become overstimulated in order to create a *psychological cocoon.* As the butterfly of your innocent nature incubates throughout the earliest years of your life, you gain personal experiences in preparation for a deeper adventure. Whether the process begins in adolescence or spontaneously unfolds in adulthood, the cocoon of incubation fulfills its mission by flaking apart through the impulse of spiritual evolution. If the purpose of the ego is to fall apart, then everything in life occurs as critical stages of development in order to usher a greater cosmic reality into view.

It's important to remember that those who haven't had flashes of transcendence aren't missing out or left behind in any way. They are just in the process of unraveling the cocoon of ego to the point where a more profound reality can be acknowledged.

Even for those who have experienced spontaneous flashes of realization, only to feel as if these experiences faded away or were somehow lost, the nervous system is simply returning to well-established patterns of conditioning. This can almost feel like you're going backward in evolution, as if everything that was so inexplicably clear when realization dawned has returned to the way things were before you began your spiritual path.

While these types of experiences can feel quite disheartening, they offer you vital feedback from your nervous system, confirming that while you may have experienced a vacation from the human condition, the patterns of overstimulation have not been fully released out of your energy field. If you were unaware of the role the nervous system plays, you might take this personally or feel like you are failing your spiritual mission.

On the other hand, once you recognize the overstimulated nervous system as the means through which life's clearest view is obscured, you travel even deeper into the grace of your journey. The further you go, the more the nervous system unravels, which gives your body permission to rest. This causes the cocoon of ego to continually flake apart, as your heart flowers open.

How Does Overstimulation Happen?

To help you understand more about how the nervous system becomes overstimulated in the first place, let's consider the behavior of babies. First, you may notice how they are already living in a state of pure consciousness. In such a state, they are constantly adjusting to sensations of a brand-new world. Every time an unrecognized possibility enters the energy field of a baby, they tend to cry. Crying doesn't necessarily suggest an experience of pain or upset, but the function of the nervous system clearing unrecognized possibilities out of the cells of the body.

In your pure state of being, sensory experiences come into your field and are immediately reflected back out in a natural rhythm. Each time this occurs, the subconscious mind is recruited to work as a recorder of patterns. Its role is to constantly track trends in your energy field while looking for ways to reduce the workload of the body. This is done so the life-force energy within your field can function at its highest level of efficiency.

Imagine a baby hears an unfamiliar sound. The sound wave immediately passes through the energy field of the baby, whose nervous system reflects it back out spontaneously. It's almost as if the baby cries to match the sound it hears. This causes the subconscious mind to notice that every time a wave is reflected out, the energy expenditure spikes. Because a baby is going to constantly respond to most experiences as unfamiliar or foreign, its subconscious mind tracks how often those spikes appear. The more often a baby responds to the multisensory nature of life, the more the nervous system steps in to reflect it back out.

This causes more energy spikes to be registered by the subconscious mind. Eventually, the subconscious mind makes a decision. Since the energy keeps spiking so often, why not make the highest point of each spike the newly conditioned state of the energy field?

This decision is made so that less energy is expended spiking up and going all the way back down to life's natural state of being.

As the spiking of energy establishes a newly conditioned state of being, your natural state is obscured as your perception of life becomes exaggerated. This invites a world of polarity, or opposites, that are seen through a lens of distortion. In a world of polarity, instead of being aware of the things you see, everything is labeled and defined in comparison to other things. From this point of reference, the miracle of existence becomes an idea called life. This is how your true nature becomes lost in the main character of a play. Throughout each scene, the innocence of your being loses touch with reality through daunting and complicated patterns of survival and is often overwhelmed by a constant state of alertness, during which the threat of deficiency and disappointment become outcomes that you regularly anticipate. This is also when the deep-rooted sense of feeling separate from love enters your reality.

Patterns of Codependency and Addiction

As this conditioned distortion sets in, the experiences coming into your field are no longer reflected back out. Instead, they are recorded into the memory of your cells. Soon, the culmination of cellular memory creates a personal sense of identity, or "I," to enhance, defend, and protect in response to others. Once the innocence of a baby becomes the conditioned temperament of a child, more cells are occupied with encoded memories to maintain the nervous system's over-stimulated state. In that level of consciousness, there are two primary patterns that are regularly acted out: codependency and addiction.

Codependency is when the quality of your experiences is dependent upon the actions or behaviors of others. It is a belief that you cannot be happy until others are satisfied and causes you to live for others while denying yourself in the process. Addiction is a habitual need for certain experiences or feelings in order to maintain a perceived sense of control in your life. The degree to which you build codependent relationships or exist in addictive behaviors suggests how overstimulated your nervous system may be.

Parents may read this and imagine that if they were able to protect their babies from this conditioning process, they could spare them from the plight of human suffering. The truth is, *each of us came to this planet for a wide spectrum of experiences* while being guided by the perfection of the Universe—from start to finish.

Equally so, having an understanding of the way in which conditioning is created never serves as a replacement for the gentleness, compassion, and loving support every child deserves.

The Path of Radical Honesty

One of the most immediate ways to unravel the nervous system is by being completely honest. Honesty is your innate ability to stand completely exposed, allowing the world to do what it may, and say what it will so that you may know who you are—beyond the realm of ideas. When there is nothing to hide or withhold, the truth is spoken freely and at no one's expense. No matter the subject of discussion, the truth contains no form of judgment. The truth celebrates how intimately you know yourself by how open and available you're willing to be. Knowing this, life's most essential wisdom always remains the same—you'll feel better once you're totally honest.

Many stray away from the value of what I call *radical honesty* out of a fear of facing the reactions of others. On a cellular level, whenever a person has an emotional reaction, their nervous system is releasing layers of conditioning. In the heart of surrender, you will see, time and time again, whatever you or anyone else is feeling is more patterns being healed.

When you are unaware of how truly healing each reaction can be, you are likely to perceive it from within the framework of ego. In ego, it's common to project blame or act out a variety of defenses toward whomever you believe is the cause of your outburst.

Due to the discomfort and inconvenient nature of certain feelings, it makes sense why so many people would hope to avoid being honest since it seems to instigate so many emotional reactions. Yet, when you know that whatever you or anyone else is feeling is a healing taking place, you are able to harmonize with the will of the Universe to consciously advance the evolution of humanity—one heart-centered interaction at a time.

Once everyday life is recognized as a playground of spiritual evolution, the real goal is learning how to courageously stand at the forefront of your own healing journey. As you accept how incredibly healing each moment can be, you are no longer obligated to judge yourself, even if failing to act in a loving manner.

No matter how much effort is exhausted, the goal of acting in a heart-centered way does not occur on a regular basis when your nervous system is overstimulated.

This is why unraveling the overstimulated nervous system in the most loving manner is the central theme of the new spiritual paradigm. By acknowledging how often the opportunity to heal yourself and others is offered throughout the play of life, your attachment to ego begins to dissolve. From that space, you are no longer victimized by reactions or in need of blaming anyone for how you feel. Equally so, you don't have to be afraid of projecting your feelings onto others since it is only likely to occur when bottling up your emotions in an attempt to hold it all in.

During the course of an emotional reaction, it may feel as if you are about to explode and cover everyone in sight with the ferocity of inner turmoil. However, if you welcome each sensation with openness and breathe into the center of whatever is felt, you can hold a sacred space for each moment of healing without being engulfed in discomfort, frustration, or pain.

When you do not openly welcome emotions, the overstimulated nervous system is fueled into greater perpetual motion. Every time someone is blamed or judged for a reaction you are having, the cells being healed are immediately filled back up with patterns of emotional debris. This can lead to future moments of emotional reaction in which life orchestrates a series of events just to help you revisit the feelings that cause you to lash out, shut down, or withdraw.

As each pattern is faced, you are liberated from tendencies to fight against the catalysts that inspire your most powerful moments of transformation. Through a renewed interest in welcoming your feelings and being honest with others, the more easily life can guide you into relationships that support your highest evolution.

While some people believe others cannot handle their truth, the honesty I am suggesting is not a weapon of any kind. Radical honesty has nothing to do with confrontation, accusation, or blame. It is an instinctive level of discernment in noticing the difference between projecting accusations and openly sharing what is felt in your experience.

Deeper Along Your Healing Journey

Another relieving aspect to radical honesty is remembering that your evolution occurs during every sincere sharing, no matter how anyone responds. This is because their response reveals what is ready to be released out of their energy field, just as your willingness to share assists in your healing as well. Whether you are being triggered or triggering another, the goal is to let go of your defenses in support of the evolution of all.

Sometimes the best support is letting someone else be heard. In other instances, it is giving someone the space they need. In whatever way it is offered, life's most inconceivable miracles enter your reality once you respect the healing journey that many don't even know is taking place.

When a discussion quickly escalates into a heated argument, the point is not a matter of agreeing or disagreeing with anyone or needing that person to validate your position. It is an opportunity to witness how cleverly everything has been orchestrated to inspire personal growth. No matter the situation, any sense of discomfort acts as a clear reminder that you are not being completely honest with yourself or others. That is because the discomfort represents cellular memories in need of being released that are held in a stagnant position through an aversion to honesty.

This emphasizes the most important meaning of the phrase "the truth shall set you free." There are many who desperately want to be set free, but not nearly as many who are willing to set themselves free by standing in the presence of truth.

Such a truth isn't initially asking you to admit anything to others but to answer the call of radical honesty by confessing the nature of your experiences to yourself. Once you've admitted the truth to yourself, your ability to intimately share with others becomes far less threatening. During any moment of honesty, you can also acknowledge the important decisions you may be avoiding that remain in your best interest to follow.

Even if your honest sharing brings relationships or career opportunities to an abrupt end, this is the grace of life's inherent perfection showing you how incredible your path is meant to be, once you're pointed in a brand-new direction. With renewed faith in the will of the Universe, the precision of integrity clears out of your way that which no longer serves you. Even if your life is turned upside down, that can only create space for greater horizons to appear.

In your own unique way, you can acknowledge radical honesty as one of the most powerful spiritual practices of the new spiritual paradigm. When you remember that *whatever you are feeling is healing,* you can rejoice in the number of times per day you are working in collaboration with the Universe to uplift the world.

For many, there is an understandable difficulty in welcoming emotions that are reminders of a painful past. You can resign yourself to embracing particular feelings, but ultimately, you cannot control whether or not your innocence feels threatened and chooses to hide. Despite how stuck you may feel, you are here to dissolve the veil of denial with the power of your own loving support.

Whether you begin with one statement of "I love you" or are able to repeat your personal love statement to yourself for a few minutes at a time, it is like reminding a child who hides in a closet that it is finally safe to come out and play. The analogy of the child is your own innocent nature hiding in the closet of your heart. Once it feels safe to come out of hiding, you are sure to regain its trust for the journey ahead.

Above and beyond any spiritual attainment, your willingness to be completely honest and loving with yourself is what reflects the maturity of an open heart. Even if you find yourself afraid to be honest, take the time to love the one who is afraid and release more cellular memory out of your energy field.

An Empathic Child

As I came to understand the inner workings of ego in adulthood, I instantly remembered myself as an empathic child. I clearly saw my young self as an "energetic sponge," sensing the unresolved emotional debris in the hearts of everyone around me. I then "saw" that as a very small child, I had made a subconscious decision: *If others seem blocked and unwilling to love me as I am, then let me replicate the conditioning I feel in their field in attempt to free their heart.*

In such an innocent way, I thought that once they were free of the conditioning I felt weighing them down, there would be nothing blocking their heart from giving me the love I so eagerly desired. Even though my intention was to take on their pain to lighten the load, I was merely replicating their perception of experiences within the cells of my body. As this process of replication occurred, I was attempting to be a perfect mirror of their conditioning, hoping that if they could see themselves reflected in me maybe they would be more emotionally open with me.

On some level, I did this to be more like the world I viewed as a way of creating resonance with the overstimulated nervous systems of those around me. I then saw how the overstimulated nervous systems of all beings created a global energy field known as the collective unconscious. This collective unconscious had manufactured a cultural sense of agreement that an overstimulated nervous system is the normal way in which human beings operate in everyday society.

As those memories continued, I saw that prior to coming to this planet and incarnating into my family, I was like an angel sent from heaven who agreed to replicate this conditioning in order to inspire greater awakening for all. I agreed to do this, so at a certain point in my evolutionary process, I would begin waking up to transmute the conditioning I had collected. Through the interconnection of One, I knew such a process of transmutation would create a ripple effect to wake up all beings in existence. I realized that I purposefully incarnated into a family to take on the conditioning they carried as a way of liberating countless lineages of conditioning throughout history that had yet to be resolved.

As I started to understand that an attachment to ego was literally as gripping and intense as one's nervous system is overstimulated, I started to recognize some very interesting connections.

When the door of your heart is closed, you tend to feel separate from the truth of your own divinity. This makes it nearly involuntary to negotiate, fight, defend, and seek ways to regularly enhance an imaginary identity of ego. With no malice toward the phenomenon of ego, I saw it as a place my innocence hid until my healing journey began.

As I learned to love what arises, I noticed how quickly my body would relax. In a state of relaxation, my innocence felt safe enough to come out of hiding. The more I relaxed, the more consciousness expanded. As this occurred, I spontaneously experienced the opening of chakras, or energy centers in the body; the activation of dormant DNA strands; the emergence of greater intuitive gifts; along with many other spiritual milestones that many pursue with exhaustion.

With the emergence of these activations that only love can inspire, I was able to harmonize with life in a way that everything seemed to conspire in my favor. It also became apparent that anything occurring in my favor was also the highest possibility for everyone around me.

From that renewed space of energetic alignment, I could manifest things just as quickly as I imagined them while drawing toward me more conscious versions of each person, even if it drastically differed from the way they acted outside of my

presence. Even throughout the various stages of enlighten-
ment and beyond, I discovered that every single goal explored
on a spiritual path effortlessly occurs as your nervous system
is unraveled—one "I love you" at a time.

As a result, the need to fight, defend, and negotiate vanished, as a heart-centered consciousness was revealed. From
that space, there was no one to wrong or any need to be right.
There was simply a willingness to notice the activity of life and
respond with love for the evolution of all.

Ending the Struggle with Discontent

What if there were no need to be right? What if you were
no longer interested in being defensive toward anyone, even
when overlooked or wrongly accused? What if instead of
focusing on what you don't have or how unfair life seems to
be, you welcomed the most incredible possibilities into your
life by opening your heart? Perhaps you might discover an
open space within each scene of your play, where there are
opportunities to act as honestly, accepting, and supportive as
only love knows how to be.

When a brand-new way of being is discovered, you are able
to see nearly every battle in life as a fight against the feeling of
discontent. An obvious sign of discontent is whenever there
is a person or circumstance that you blame for any experience.

In fact, simply by surrendering the tendency to blame
throughout stressful or painful situations, you may experience far less pain and stress along the way. This helps to free
you from the pitfalls of suffering instead of perpetuating it
through defensive behavior. It's normal to oppose discontent

when it can be seen as exactly the way you don't wish to feel. Yet, it is the impulse to deny, avoid, shut down, or lash out against any perceivable cause that prevents you from discovering something more meaningful about it.

A Compulsive Pattern of Seeking

Underneath the feeling of discontent is a compulsive pattern of seeking. Within this subconscious pattern, there is an impulse to seek out more of something in an attempt to avoid the despair of having less. For example, many people believe they will have less anxiety as long as they seek out more forms of security. It's as if the ego believes, "If I add more things to my collection, the inevitability of loss won't sting so much."

The subconscious pattern of needing to gain something in an attempt to avoid the pain of having less is woven throughout the fabric of society. Perhaps someone who grows frustrated with their career makes a drastic move around the globe to an exotic new country. Shortly after their arrival, the new location doesn't feel as new anymore as the ego looks in alternative directions for additional forms of reinvention.

Maybe in the aftermath of losing a loved one, an ego suppresses its pain by purchasing luxury items or tries reliving the past to remember a time when life was happier.

Of course, not every decision or purchase suggests an ego at play. It's the beliefs you have about your choices or the hope of what such things will bring you that indicate whether an ego is collecting more as a remedy for having less.

Even on a spiritual path, the tendency to seek, as a way of trying to resolve the feeling of discontent, acts as a telltale sign of how overstimulated a nervous system happens to be. In some instances, ego can use a spiritual path to seek more clarity in hopes of having less confusion. That can even be an aspiration of the highest order to seek more liberation as a way of suffering less often. The ego can also rearrange the polarity of more or less by trying to have fewer thoughts or less fear as a way of creating more peace of mind.

While nearly any aspect of life can be a way for the ego to reinvent itself, even adopting a new and improved spiritual persona along the way, the one thing ego cannot use for perpetual reinvention is love. That is because love is a high vibrational energy that directly addresses the source of ego.

When love is invited into your life, it unravels the subconscious patterns that keep you so dissatisfied through a constant need to seek. This means you don't have to exhaust yourself by living under a spiritual microscope. Instead, you can make opening your heart your central point of focus and allow love to find a way to resolve it all for you.

The Cycle of Acquisition and Elimination

When the nervous system is overstimulated, the ego oscillates between cycles of acquisition and elimination. First, it seeks out *more in an attempt to be farther away from the perceived hardship of less.* Once it has satisfied a momentary hunger for more, it inevitably switches gears and uses the same seeking energy to eliminate things from its life.

An example of this could be an insatiable desire for a soul mate relationship that is believed to be the remedy for loneliness. More often than not, the one seeking such a partner finds one. Maybe the romance lasts weeks, months, or even years, until the one who pursued a relationship so passionately now believes their happiness will be found in being single. Once they are single and available, they soon explore the possibilities of finding a different partner, repeating the same pattern no matter how long the new relationship may or may not last.

Of course, there are also people in relationships who would be much happier if they left, but when the cycle of acquisition and elimination continues in such a predictable, repetitive manner, it might be time to take a closer look at the forces that influence you.

You might even be reading this and thinking, *I've become aware of these patterns and cycles, which is why I'm on a spiritual path attempting to resolve them.* This can get even more frustrating when the very path you pursue to address the issues of the ego becomes a new way for the ego to reinvent itself.

It can also become more complicated if a spiritual path teaches you to monitor or oppose your ego only to create a new spiritual persona that patrols your psyche to make sure no ego makes an appearance.

Instead of overwhelming yourself by trying to keep it all straight or working so hard to do the right thing, I invite you to immerse yourself in love—no matter how many patterns, beliefs, judgments, or self-defeating habits remain active in you. The fact that you are here reading these words offers renewed hope that life is pointing you in a direction where your greatest success is ensured.

By loving the one who can't do anything right, loving the one who feels like a failure, or even loving the one who is burdened by discontent, you immediately turn a corner in the direction of true heartfelt relief. This is why I say you always deserve more love, not less. By offering more love to your true innocent nature on a regular basis, the measurements of gains and losses, along with the patterns of acquisition and elimination quickly fall apart.

In essence, being caught in patterns of ego creates the very discontent that an ego is trying to resolve. That is, until you directly address the core of human suffering by returning to love—once and for all.

Once you recognize each compulsion for more of this or less of that as ways in which your inner child cries out for love, a world of pain, stress, injustice, and antagonism becomes a reality of peace, freedom, inspiration, and joy.

The Overactive Mind

IN THE PRACTICE of loving what arises, the heart isn't always the part of the body calling out for your attention. While the heart can always remain your central point of focus, it is helpful to unravel the nervous system by sending love to an overactive mind. As your life experiences may reveal, your mind may be as noisy as your heart is closed. By allowing the mind to be embraced as a child in need of kindness, support, acceptance, and attention, you are able to end each conflict within yourself by honoring the one who cannot be silenced any longer. Many have turned their mind into battlefields in response to the hurtful, destructive, or even judgmental thoughts that consume their attention.

While it makes sense to imagine how peaceful your mind would become if only you could unplug it from the outlet, the mind only remains overactive as an attention-seeking device the Universe uses to help you return to love.

Whether or not you enjoy or agree with your mind has really nothing to do with why it's overactive or consumed in doubt, fear, pain, or judgment. Spirituality should never be confused with obedience training. Your goal is not to wrestle your mind into submission or pry your heart open with any degree of force. The invitation that has been sent your way is to recognize everything, including the activity of your mind, as an opportunity to love. You can think of incessant mental noise as an alarm clock. Its purpose is to wake you up by reminding you of the perfect moment to embrace your mind with unwavering heartfelt support.

From this deeper space of harmony, you are not blaming the mind but responding to it in the way that love would reach out to a five-year-old in pain. As I often say, if it's not the way you would talk to a child in need, it shouldn't be the way you talk to yourself.

As you engage with your mind, like a parent consoling a child, a feeling of safety allows your heart to expand. Once the alarm clock of your mind has done its job by properly informing you of the next one in line to be loved, it becomes silent until another reminder is needed.

Just as you don't have to anticipate running out of gas because there is a gauge in your car to track the level available, there is no reason to stress or worry about loving yourself when emotional reactions or an overactive mind already act as the perfect signals to alert you.

Above and beyond any degree of understanding, the greatest demonstration of your true divine nature is a body that feels safe enough to participate in life with openness and enthusiasm. When you have aligned with the most exciting possibilities that have been awaiting your arrival, you remain relaxed and responsive, no matter how tumultuous the world appears to be or how triggered anyone becomes.

Discovering Safety by Slowing Your Breath

Another sign of an overstimulated nervous system is shallow breathing. Just as the mind is as noisy as the heart is closed, the breath is as shallow as the nervous system is overstimulated. As your breath slows and deepens, the mind is returned to silence while the heart is permitted to open. Simply by taking several mini-breathing breaks throughout the day, you cultivate an ability to feel instinctively safe wherever you go.

Let us explore the breath as a potent healing exercise:

> If you're unsure how to slow or deepen your breath, just inhale through your nostrils in a more relaxed way than usual. It might feel like you are taking the time to savor the in-breath as if there's something fragrant to smell. Notice how the breath instinctively slows when your inhale is drawn inward like a sweet aroma. Once your inhale reaches its natural peak, simply pause for a moment, and then let the breath out gently through your mouth. You can imagine the exhale like a child slowly blowing bubbles out through a drinking straw. Again, draw the breath in through your nostrils, hold it for just one moment, and then exhale gently through your mouth.

By breathing in through your nostrils, you welcome in the delicious fragrance of your divinity, holding the breath for a moment to savor the magnificence of life and then letting it out as blessings of compassion, joy, and ease for one and all. As your breath slows, you are liberated from any tendency to control the behavior of others, no longer insisting that harmony is when people match your vibration of consciousness.

Requiring anyone to meet you where you are is an easy way to forget the unique journey of others. While you may have encountered obstacles that were easy for you to face, these same obstacles could be insurmountable challenges in someone else's life. While it is understandable to desire someone else to meet you at a complimentary frequency in order to connect, it's important to take the time to breathe slower than they are breathing so that you are able to experience your own vibration of consciousness instead of being sucked into their unresolved patterns.

An easy way to recognize the speed of someone's breath is by listening to how quickly they speak. Shallow breathing tends to elicit fast-talking as well as a lack of enunciation. By slowing down the pace of your words, you are freed from needing to rush sentences together in an attempt to have a final say. When in the presence of someone who seems defensive, distracted, or unable to meet you in an open-hearted manner, just speak more slowly and breathe more deeply to become a better listener in their life than they may be for themselves.

The greater interest you show in others, without needing to interrupt anything they say, the more you allow them to feel authentically seen and heard. This increases the likelihood that they will find the motivation to hear and see themselves more often.

It is important to remember that no one is capable of taking a genuine interest in you until they've become the one who offers themselves the support, kindness, and care they yearn to discover. This helps you see your interactions with others as opportunities to slow your breath and practice the act of listening as an engaged form of meditation.

Equally so, your response to what anyone says offers additional chances to speak out loud the words you've always wanted to hear.

Even when someone else's life circumstances do not match your history of experiences, there is always common ground discovered on an emotional level. Instead of focusing on how different they seem from you, take the time to ask yourself: "What do I emotionally feel in their presence? Can I remember a time when I felt that way? If so, what are the words I wish someone had been able to say to me that would've made me feel so much better? Can I be the one who offers those words as a chance to heal both hearts?"

No matter how anyone responds to your kindness, just by repeating out loud the words you didn't hear often enough or never heard at all, you guarantee yourself to be the one who exits each scene of life more healed, aligned, and expanded than the moment before.

By savoring your words, slowing down your breath, listening with greater interest, and gifting others with your personal love statement, you anchor a higher vibration of consciousness. As that occurs, you invite the subconscious mind of another to do their best to match your frequency instead of getting pulled into its patterns by unknowingly matching the speed of their words or shallowness of their breath.

This is why many conversations quickly escalate into misunderstandings. When conflict arises, two people often wrestle for dominant positions through accusations and demands. Along a heart-centered path, a conversation is an opportunity to be more aligned with your true innocent nature. It is a chance to practice speaking to others the words you'd like to hear more often and listening at a deeper level than others may have heard you before.

Because your subconscious mind doesn't recognize the difference between the words you say to yourself and the words you speak to another, conversations become an essential way to rewrite your inner programming while gifting others with the compliments that support their healing.

Whether you're engaging with children, interacting with relatives, or meeting the ongoing demands of work, each environment has been created by the Universe to help you transform so you can live in harmony, as the love that you are.

Guided by the Law of Polarity

One of the most effective ways to raise the vibration of your relationships is to engage the law of polarity. Through this universal principle, you are able to better understand the balance of opposing forces. Instead of matching the energy of others, you merely do the opposite. If others shout, you choose to listen. Since shouting can only occur through shallow breathing, you slow down and calm your breath. When others are tense and rigid, you relax your body. If others complain, you respond with a compliment. Even if you feel dominated by the energy, words, or actions of another, the law of polarity inspires you to back away and give them more time and space so they can be with themselves on a more intimate level.

By learning to do the opposite whenever stress, pain, or blame arises, you are holding a sacred space for every heart during life's most critical moments of healing.

This also helps you learn that you don't need anyone to act in a certain way in order to feel the harmony, bliss, and joy that life always provides. While it makes sense that a partner is the one who supports you the most and offers you all the love you could ever need, the difference between feeling seen or ignored is more so a reflection of how often you love your own heart.

It is common to unknowingly ignore the requests from your own innocent nature while waiting for a partner to treat you better. When this tendency influences you, there are endless ways in which you envision everyone becoming better characters in your life, if only they would listen more intently or learn to act differently.

When the demands you have in each relationship inspire you to be the one who acts upon them, the law of polarity assists you in finding space to gift yourself and others with the nurturing support and engaged listening that no amount of negotiating with others can ever guarantee. While such a universal law has the potential to shift relationships into greater depths of intimacy, it is never intended to be used as a way of loving yourself privately while hiding from a relationship you are completely afraid to end.

Often, as energetically sensitive souls, we can be more focused on other people's feelings or reactions than following the wisdom of our own inner guidance. There can even be a belief that says "It's not a conscious break-up until they are okay with setting me free."

There can be such a fear of hurting another or being the contributing factor to someone else's despair that you unknowingly stay in broken relationships, not seeing how the most loving thing for both hearts is to go your own way. No matter how anyone responds when your highest truth is spoken, each moment of sharing acts as catalysts of spiritual growth for the evolution of everyone involved.

Spiritual Codependency

It can be normal for energetically sensitive souls to linger in outdated relationships in an attempt to help others process the pain of loss. No matter how attached you are to another person or how deeply that person clings to you, such a dynamic only invites more toxicity until you are able to walk away and make time for the innocence that calls out for your attention.

No matter the time or energy invested in any relationship, the law of polarity allows you to hold sacred space for the healing of any heart without getting lost in spiritual codependency. This frees you from the tendency to stall your own evolution by waiting for others to be okay with the choices that may only feel right for you. Even when a choice that appears so right to you seems to hurt another, this is the humbling nature of life's most profound healing being revealed. Despite how badly you feel for someone else's pain, there is no reason to feel guilty when only gifts of expansion are given. Even when you don't know how to be okay with decisions that others reject, that becomes a life-changing opportunity to follow through with your inner guidance while welcoming codependency as the next one in line to be loved.

It is vital to remember you are never turning your back on anyone; you are merely facing in the direction of your highest potential. While it may feel as if you are abandoning someone in their most dire moment of despair, you are being guided by the Universe to give proper distance, which for many people, is the only way to turn inward and discover their innocence at a greater spiritual level.

Through the law of polarity, you come to notice every single character who enters your reality is an animated flash card of personal growth. Each one helps bring this cosmic principle to life by inspiring you to do the opposite in response to those who lash out or shut down. Each of those personal encounters becomes an invitation to breathe more slowly, speak more softly, and act more graciously as a way of coming into greater harmony with the light of your divinity. This allows you to feel safe in your body, not as a result of personal circumstances, but based on how compassionately you are willing to respond to the situations at hand.

It's as if your innocence only understands the world you see based on your responses and reactions to it. Despite how anyone around you chooses to be, the difference between perceiving a life of synchronicity versus a world of endless stress solely depends on how you speak, breathe, and move—from one moment to the next.

Exploring the Ego

WHEN YOU WAKE UP out of ego, it is not as if there is some "thing" you have actually transcended. Instead, you see through the façade of everything you've assumed or have been taught about your ego. The recurring theme in a spiritual journey is awakening out of every conclusion, belief, and reference point, including those created out of your most-treasured moments of clarity. This occurs at every stage of exploration until only the truth of love remains. Since everything but love is relinquished, why not put aside any insight, practice, or course of study by allowing your heart to lead the way?

While ego is the imaginary identity of an overstimulated nervous system, it's important to provide a more practical understanding of what this actually means. When rooted in a heart-centered journey, you are able to make sense of your life, but in a way in which nothing needs to be admonished, punished, persecuted, abandoned, or avoided in the name of your highest spiritual growth. This is not to say that what you've learned about the ego from traditional paths is incorrect. It's more about that you have arrived at an exciting point in history where you are ready to expand your understanding of ego in a more universal way.

In many traditions, ego is viewed as the personality of the body. Through helping many people cross over into the afterlife, as well as through communication with those who are already on the other side, I've discovered that the personality goes way beyond the boundaries of the body, as an aspect of the soul.

The personality is an individuated expression of eternal light, celebrating the uniqueness of divinity in form. In my experience of communicating with beings after they've crossed over into the afterlife, they appear to me still in the shape and form of the person from their human incarnation. In some inexplicable way, when I am able to connect with their consciousness, I converse with the essence of a soul just as you would have a conversation on the phone. In the beginning I thought it was just my imagination, but when the messages that were conveyed to me were validated by their loved ones, it helped cultivate a wellspring of respect for the endless potential and magnificent capabilities that dwell within each of us. During my conversations with souls, they appeared with the same personality traits, quirkiness, and humor they embodied when they were here in form, but within a larger context of what they may not have been aware of during their lifetime.

By understanding the personality as an aspect of the soul, it liberates you from being ashamed of your traits and characteristics. No matter how far you travel in your spiritual journey, your unique qualities are not eliminated by evolution but enhanced to their highest potential at the rate of your expansion.

You are not here to achieve a state of transcendence in which you have no personality—because not having one would effectively deny the very uniqueness that you are bringing to the world. Everyone has a unique personality, which carries a one-of-a-kind vibrational frequency that no one else in history can deliver to this planet. Like a color of a rainbow that no one else can illuminate through the beauty of your being, you are bringing to life a special remembrance of truth as a gift provided for all. Even if you are dwelling in a personality that feels limiting or painful, you are working on behalf of the Universe to explore this side of the emotional scale to build up momentum and catapult into higher vibrations of conscious expression.

No matter how low you go into the agony of victimhood, this is only part of a miraculous journey where you rise out of the ashes of fear, shame, and regret to shine a light that heals every heart.

When Personalities Become Inflamed

If reality is like an ocean with the waves representing various personalities that crash and collide from one interaction to the next, you realize that both the ocean and the waves are equally a part of one eternal truth. If you hold a more classical definition of ego as the personality of body, you may assume the ocean must become void of waves in order to be what it already is. Just like waves cannot crash or collide in such a way that will cause the ocean to drown, your personality is never in the way of recognizing a truth that always exists within you. This helps you understand the nature of ego as a conditioned tendency to be lost in an inflamed personality structure due to an overstimulated nervous system.

Typically, the word *inflammation* is associated with the different ways that bodies respond to their environment. This can include reactions to certain types of food in which allergens are capable of producing an inflammatory or toxic response in the body. Ego is what happens when the personality gets inflamed. For example, when you see someone who is angry, they are in a state of emotional inflammation. To say that they're in ego may be a true statement, but through the eyes of the Universe, you are able to see how they are having an "allergic reaction" to their conditioned state of being. This means ego is much like an allergy toward the unconsciousness that each of us came here to resolve. When the ego is active, the innocence within you, or within anyone else, exists in an exaggerated manner. As you love what arises, you heal your vibrational allergies to joyfully live on an evolving planet, no matter how quickly or slowly others around you seem to grow.

When you start to see ego as the inflammation of the personality, you notice how often you can become "puffed up." Whether puffed up in righteousness, defensive postures, or in response to the evidence of injustice, an inflamed personality creates an exaggerated perception of life. When living with an allergic reaction to the vibration of the planet, an exaggerated level of consciousness causes you to oscillate between spiritual highs and emotional lows. This can create much suffering until you cultivate love as a potent form of energy medicine to return your personality to its original form.

Four Types of Inflammation

While intuitively guided in my exploration of ego, I've come to recognize four basic types of inflammation. The first one is called *righteous inflammation*. It is characterized by an ego structure that feeds on needing to always be right by making others wrong. Even in the presence of one who is saying something totally correct, the ego that is righteously inflamed must make another point in an attempt to be even more right than the other. This type of ego lives to have the upper hand and final word—even if both parties agree on the topic at hand. The theme of righteous inflammation is, "I'm always right."

One of the aspects of a righteous ego is *skepticism*. This occurs when an ego is convinced that the way it sees the world is the way everyone else should see it. In an attempt to subconsciously keep the inflammation of righteousness alive and active, this person remains skeptical of anything other than their specific point of view.

The second type of inflamed ego is called *victimized inflammation*. This is the kind of inflammation in which an ego believes it is always a victim of circumstances. From this perception, even when life seems to be going right, something always happens to turn it upside down. A victimized ego holds very tightly to its judgments, beliefs, and opinions as the reasons their life is regularly in chaos. This type of inflammation is commonly fed by beliefs in superstition. Oftentimes, the more spiritually themed a superstition happens to be, the more it inflames this type of ego structure. Whether a belief in light versus dark or pitting good against bad, a victimized ego typically acts as an instigator of turmoil that is guaranteed to be hurt or heartbroken by the way others respond to it.

Even if others do not respond at all, a victimized ego uses such feedback to feel invisible or inferior to the world around it.

When caught in the inflammation of victimhood, it is quite difficult, though not impossible, to see your circumstances as divine catalysts of universal will. A victimized ego cannot grasp that everything in reality is there to help it transform. This is because a victimized ego is fueled by stagnation, refusing to grow in a world of endless change.

If the theme of righteous inflammation is "I'm always right," then the theme of a victimized ego is "Life isn't fair." When in the grip of victimized inflammation, everyone and everything outside of you is the source of your pain, which prevents a larger cosmic picture from being recognized.

The third type of inflammation is called *entitled inflammation*. This occurs when a person believes it is their right to have whatever they want, exactly when they want it, even at the expense or to the detriment of others. Of course, there is nothing inherently wrong or problematic in believing that you are worthy of receiving all that you desire since worthiness is an aspect of your highest truth. However, when the personality becomes inflamed, an innate sense of worthiness becomes exaggerated. In entitled inflammation, the ego tends to believe that everyone must fulfill their every whim and demand with little to no regard for the well-being of other people's experiences. As you can imagine, the theme of an entitled ego is "What about me?" Even when served by others, there is never an end to the requests and demands of an ego that believes it controls the characters in its life.

The fourth type of inflammation is called *needy inflammation*. In this type of ego, no matter how much attention is received from others, it never feels like enough to be properly filled up. Despite how intently someone listens, there is always a lingering sense of being invisible, unrecognized, undervalued, or unheard. In needy inflammation, it's easy to feel misunderstood. No matter how much time, interest, and attention you receive from others, it only makes this type of ego hungry for more.

Whether active in you or someone you know, needy inflammation can be quite draining for those held in the grip of it. Needy inflammation brings to life the true meaning of the term "energy vampire." When inflamed in this way, no matter how much reassurance you get from others, you are always afraid of being abandoned, left out, or losing everything you've been given. As a result, the theme of needy inflammation is "It's never enough."

While you may recognize yourself or others in these descriptions, it is common to embody combinations of those aspects or to flow in and out like the changing of weather patterns. I've even seen ego structures that are combinations of all four aspects at once. Even at that stage of inflammation, there is always a possibility of true heartfelt relief when loving yourself becomes your recurring response to any question or concern.

In each of these aspects of inflammation, there is always a kernel of truth. However, when your personality gets inflamed, things get quite exaggerated. For example, in the natural state of your true innocent nature, it is not righteousness but rather the wisdom of the Universe that wishes to spare others undue suffering by providing insights that could help change their lives. Having a desire to point someone in a better direction as a way of assisting in their journey is a wonderfully inspired impulse. Yet, when your personality is inflamed, you go from wanting to uplift the lives of others to always needing to be right by making another wrong in the process.

Even in victimized inflammation, there is truth to the experience of feeling as if everything is personally happening to you. This is a reflection of your true innocent nature experiencing the ups and downs of life from a close, intimate perspective. It's always important to remember that your seat in the theater of life is within the body of the main character. This means your front row seat exists as "I AM." There is, in fact, some truth to the direct experience that everything happens to you. However, when the personality is inflamed and your perception of life is exaggerated, it appears as if everything in the world is conspiring against you in a relentless and overwhelming way.

Equally with entitled inflammation, when rooted in your natural state of innocence, it is under the power of your own divine authority to receive all that you dream, wish, and desire. In every breath, you have every right to have more prosperity than can ever be imagined, to have fulfilling committed relationships, to travel around the world, and to see the most breathtaking creations that have ever materialized into form. In your natural state, there is a healthy level of cosmic confidence that allows you to stand tall and fully own your life as a unique expression of spirit in action. Yet, when your personality gets inflamed and your view of life becomes exaggerated, the innate confidence of being worthy becomes an imbalanced desire for the world to work for you at anyone's expense.

Even in needy inflammation, there is also a truth to be seen. At the core of your being, there is a deep-rooted desire to connect with others as unique ways of encountering your own divinity in different forms. There is a desire to connect, to be heard, to hear others, and to express uniqueness throughout your life. But when your personality becomes inflamed, a desire to express and connect becomes neediness, an inferno of hunger that cannot be extinguished. No matter how much is received from others, only more desperation is created when the personality is inflamed.

By exploring ego in a more heart-centered way, you can have greater patience and compassion throughout your daily encounters. Instead of ridiculing or persecuting the characters within your life, you will be able to see the light of divinity dancing in a play of exaggerated perception. While the ability to see at this cosmic level may be limited by an inflamed personality, any amount of time spent incubating in a cocoon of ego prepares you to awaken a greater truth for all.

The Calamity of Comparison

Even though the ego is a byproduct of an overstimulated nervous system, it may be easier to understand it as an inflamed personality structure. To walk around asking yourself whether your nervous system is overstimulated may not be as effective as recognizing throughout the day the moments when your personality becomes inflamed. When this occurs, whether momentarily or over a long period of time, you tend to perceive life through an exaggerated lens. This causes you to interpret the world through categories of distinction. As your view is obscured through judgments or comparison, there is an unconscious tendency to define things as either good or bad, less and more, or even light versus dark.

While the act of comparing is natural in modern-day society, it doesn't necessarily make life any clearer when everything in view is stringently defined by similarities or differences to other things. Imagine liking someone because of the ways they remind you of people you admire. Instead of embracing their attributes as an individual, they are either accepted or rejected based on who they resemble in your experience.

There are even TV sitcoms highlighting the calamity of comparison in hilarious fashion. One example may depict a main character who finally meets the woman of his dreams but is then tortured by the fact that she shares the same name as his mother. Now every time they are together, his ego believes he is on a date with his mom. Perhaps as the main character attempts to put the association with his mother aside, the woman of his dreams says familiar phrases that cause him to imagine his mother's face on her body. This occurs routinely until the character cannot take it anymore, much to the amusement of the audience.

Another example commonly seen on sitcoms is creating tension between a main character and a close ally who unknowingly befriends the main character's secret arch nemesis. This sets the stage for the main character to give their ally an ultimatum: either to help them seek zany forms of revenge against their sworn enemy or become another enemy of theirs. While it is easy to be entertained by the embellished actions of TV characters through situations their egos create, it is far more painful when a tendency to view life through veils of comparison remain unnoticed in you.

When the personality is inflamed, you can become territorial with the people, places, and things that define your sense of worth. While this can make you an ally to those close to you, it can equally create endless enemies out of those who unknowingly invade your territory. Whether it's competing with new characters at work, feeling even worse about your favorite team losing on home turf, or judging others in response to how those you love have been mistreated, the territorial nature of ego can be easily overlooked when confused with the value of loyalty.

While it's wonderful to be a loyal supporter, this becomes more like a territorial power play when you stand up for something that causes you to lash out at others whom you perceive are on the opposite "side." Even if playing the role of a supporter, when someone you love is heartbroken, you cannot assist in their healing by adding more judgment toward the person in question.

When your personality is inflamed, a willingness to love quickly becomes an impulse to blame in response to the way you or someone else is feeling. Because ego can only exist as an inflamed personality for as long as the nervous system is overstimulated, it cannot see life as fresh opportunities that don't have to be like or unlike anything else.

As your nervous system unravels out of patterns of overstimulation, there is no instinct to judge through comparing or contrasting at all. Instead, there is more an innate willingness to welcome each day as its own incarnation of brand-new experiences. Even when those in your life are facing the despair of adversity, there is no need to adopt their enemies as your own in order to listen, support, and encourage them through an unexpected moment of change. When your nervous system is relaxed, you resonate with encouraging others as they heal instead of igniting the fire of antagonism.

No matter how betrayed or heartbroken anyone seems to be, there is no healing when time is spent assembling an army to judge or persecute the ones who seem to cause such pain. While there can be a false sense of power in bringing egos together with a common enemy to take down, your world cannot become a peaceful, joyful, and happy place to be until a tendency to fight becomes an opportunity to uplift those who are hurting. This occurs by loving what arises. Whether loving the one in pain, accepting the one who desires revenge, forgiving the one who is good at holding grudges, or having compassion for the one who seeks conflict in an attempt to have the final word, each aspect is only here to be acknowledged as never before.

No matter how righteous, victimized, entitled, or needy you or anyone else remains, this merely reveals a world that you came to transform through the grace of an open heart.

Love as the Dissolver of Inflammation

Despite how unreasonable people may act when lost in ego, your personality can be equally triggered into various states of inflammation when judgment is your response to any personal encounter. Whether disappointed by the lack of support in your life or imagining your happiness as the end result of others behaving differently, those situations provide opportunities to further your own love revolution.

Such a revolution occurs by remembering, *I'm the one who deserves more love, not less, no matter how disappointed, angry, or insistent I am in needing others to change. Each feeling is here to be loved as only I can love it.*

No matter how many times a day your personality is inflamed or how often your actions and words are motivated by ego, the objective isn't to judge yourself when you become triggered. Instead, you are cultivating an awareness of how many times throughout the day your insistence, temper, rigidity, and demands for external support become invitations to love yourself more often.

Even when you find yourself inundated by the demands of your job or under an intense deadline, it can be easy to be more concerned with accomplishing an end result than tuning in to the wisdom of your body. When you are inflamed, you can feel as if you're under constant pressure in a race against time.

While it can be easy to point the finger of blame at the relentless demands of life, perhaps your circumstances only seem so overwhelming when your nervous system is overstimulated.

What if opening your heart during the heat of the moment allowed challenges or deadlines to become exciting instead of daunting?

In order to call upon your highest qualities for the well-being of all, it is essential to become the source of your own fulfillment. No matter how consistently you're operating from ego, such moments invite you to realize, *I'm not here to ridicule myself or anyone else's behavior. I deserve more love, not less.*

In order to embody this truth as a brand-new way of being, I invite you to repeat the following healing mantra:

Whenever righteousness arises, it is here to
    be loved, as only I can love it.

When victimhood is apparent, it is here to
    be loved, as only I can love it.

When entitlement arises, it is here to be loved,
    as only I can love it.

When neediness remains, it is here to be loved,
    as only I can love it.

When the finger of blame points in any
    direction or is turned on myself, it is here
    to be loved, as only I can love it.

When I am inundated by the stress, pressure,
    expectations, and obligations of any role or
    responsibility that I am playing out in my
    family, occupation, or in any relationship, it
    is only here to be loved, as only I can love it.

When the need for more, the fear of less, the
    need for less, or even the fear of more cloud
    the clarity of my highest wisdom, it is here
    to be loved, as only I can love it.

Even when I'm feeling guilty, ashamed, hopeless,
    withdrawn, uninspired, apathetic, judgmental,
    cruel, heartless, insincere, spiteful, dishonest,

callous, pessimistic, passive-aggressive, or even sarcastic, even all of that is here to be loved, as only I can love it.

The Clearing of All Karmic Agreements

Through interacting with those souls in the afterlife, one of the most interesting things I've experienced is a soul telling me how much it was run by guilt and obligation during an incarnation. I have often heard, "I remember making agreements in many different lifetimes. I punished and judged myself for trying to measure up to those agreements."

As they were able to see life from a much broader perspective, their guilt and judgment vanished. I've often heard them say, "I now see that I never would have measured up to those agreements. All they were meant to do is to keep me occupied in the very structure that motivated me to search for ways out. Now that I am free, I see those agreements were never made by me. They were things I agreed to when I wasn't in my right mind."

From working with many individuals who are dealing with agreements that have been made in various lifetimes, I have seen firsthand the benefits of clearing such agreements. Any agreement you've negotiated was most likely created by ego. When your personality is no longer inflamed, you are not subject to the terms and conditions of an agreement. This essentially means that once each agreement made by ego is nullified, you are no longer stifled by the gravity of obligation. In the absence of obligation, you can freely make decisions and even create new agreements from the freedom and will of your own divine authority. Since the agreements made by ego were done in an attempt to guarantee outcomes that have already been orchestrated by the Universe, they have no benefit other than offering relief once they are cleared.

To experience freedom from any degree of obligation, please repeat the following healing mantra:

> Whether from this lifetime or any incarnation throughout, I clear, unravel, nullify, and transmute any agreements, contracts, energy cords, imprints, or attachments that I have accepted through obligation, conformity, manipulation, fear, or in an attempt to control the fate of a particular outcome in life. I hereby release these agreements, contracts, cords, imprints, and attachments for the healing, awakening, and transformation of one and all. As of this moment, I am free and clear to make decisions from the freedom and will of my highest divine authority through the power reclaimed as I AM now. And so it is.

It is also common for empaths to carry over outdated vows from being monks and nuns in past lifetimes, including the bodhisattva vow itself. The bodhisattva vow can be misinterpreted to suggest not leaving this Earth plane until all beings are liberated, awake, and free from suffering. When taken at face value, it often cultivates righteous inflammation through a belief in spiritual martyrdom. The true essence of the bodhisattva vow is not a promise to keep but an aspiration to fulfill. In becoming what seems like the first person in the world to stand tall in the beauty of your eternal radiance, you cultivate a vibration of heart-centered consciousness.

The spiritual aspiration honored in a bodhisattva vow can often be depicted through the relationship between flowers and seeds. Just as a seed already exists as the potential of a flower, it must be grounded and exposed to the elements of nature in order to sprout roots and blossom into form. While seeds exist as the potential of flowers, they cannot sense the ecstasy of their own fragrance and release this perfume throughout the garden of humanity until they have come into bloom.

To celebrate your willingness to blossom, as a way of assisting all seeds throughout the cycles of growth, it is important to release even the formal spiritual vows unknowingly made under the influence of an inflamed personality. While such vows were well intended, they most likely have kept you occupied in a spiritual ego, which can stunt the growth of your evolution. It's not as if any particular vow didn't have a purpose at the time they were taken. It's that releasing them celebrates the fulfillment of their role that cannot assist you any further until they are released.

Even when you believe that you are coming from the purest heart-centered space, there is one key point that reminds you that only egos negotiate such agreements or take on any vow.

In every spiritual agreement or vow, there is a perception that you are making a commitment to the Universe as if you are someone or something other than the Universe in form. While an agreement can be made by a seed, that agreement is no longer valid to the reality of a flower. In order to transform seeds of divinity into flowers of truth, every vow or agreement that binds you must be resolved.

Even when an agreement is made between two people, they are often agreeing to terms and conditions as if each person is something other than the Universe appearing in form. If both are rooted in knowing themselves as the totality of all, no need for an agreement would even arise. This is much like your fingers not needing to make agreements with one another in order to work together as a hand. Whether it is a child agreeing to the demands of a parent as a way of avoiding further punishment or hoping to earn their way into more loving approval, this kind of agreement often occurs in a state of duress.

Knowing myself to have been a Tibetan monk from past lifetimes, I acknowledge the vows taken as some of the most beautiful declarations in existence. And yet, those vows were declared as something other than the Universe, either as a character or agreements between characters, as a way of negotiating terms and conditions within a Universe.

It's not as if you shouldn't have ever made the vow or agreed to its terms, but it's more a sign of the times throughout an evolving planet. As beings evolve, so must the spiritual paths that hope to inspire growth and expansion for those who yearn to awaken.

Through these words, I can confirm that you have arrived at an exciting point in history. You have successfully fulfilled the aspirations of your deepest spiritual impulse. Through the experiences you have survived up to this point, you have completed every requirement that any agreement or vow brought your way. In celebrating a graduation into a new level of consciousness, it is time to lighten the load and free yourself of the past so you can enter this moment—fresh, renewed, and reborn. As you begin to see this moment as a spiritually aligned newborn, you bring to life the harmony of a brand-new reality.

In honor of taking such a courageous step into the heart of surrender than ever before, I invite you to repeat the following healing mantra:

As the master of my destiny and the creator of my reality, I accept that all contracts, agreements, and every formal vow that I have made were not made by the truth that I AM. They were agreed upon by an inflamed personality structure that I thought I was, but I now realize is not the highest truth of my being.

I accept that neither the Universe nor my highest truth would ever or could ever hold me accountable to agreements made when innocently lost in exaggerated states of unconsciousness. I accept that I wasn't wrong to take on such vows or make any agreements. These were part of a divine plan for me to incarnate into a world in which contracts, vows, and agreements were already in place. As I take the time to nullify them, I free myself and the world in the process.

In knowing what I now know, I hereby nullify all contracts and agreements, known and unknown, seen or unseen, remembered and forgotten, throughout all cellular memory and my subconscious mind. I also release, relinquish, and surrender all formal vows I may have made as a monk or a nun. This includes the vow of poverty, the vow of chastity, the vow of renunciation, the vow of silence, and all misunderstood bodhisattva vows, agreements of victimhood, codependency, and martyrdom, as well as anything else believed, imagined, agreed to, or assumed by ego.

By the appointment of my own divine authority, I allow these vows to be cleared and released out of this energy field, returned to the Source of their origin, transmuted completely, and returned to the purity, wholeness, and perfection of eternal light. As of this moment, I reclaim my complete and absolute power, allowing this personality to uniquely express the light of divinity that completes the mission I came here to fulfill. From this moment forward, I activate and embody a new heart-centered consciousness that heals, awakens, rebirths, and liberates all as I AM now. And so it is.

Freedom from the Four Types of Inflammation

By clearing agreements, contracts, and vows, you help free your personality from the four types of inflammation. For example, as you clear the formal vows of being a monk or nun that many empaths carry in the cells of their body, the personality is liberated from the identities of righteous and entitled inflammation. This allows you to rest in the humility of your heart without needing to be restricted by the framework of a specific role. In doing so, you no longer require a world to suffer in pain in order to provide you with an opportunity to share your gifts. Instead, you offer the magnificence of every gift that assists the world in evolving into higher levels of consciousness without needing anyone to suffer along the way. As agreements are released, including bonds to those who may have hurt, abandoned, or betrayed you, there is no longer a tendency to define yourself by a past you were always meant to survive.

While many agreements are meant to be cleared, it is not necessary to clear *every vow* throughout your life. If you are blessed to be in a beautifully committed relationship or marriage where vows were taken as a conscious choice in celebration of love, those can only support your spiritual evolution. At the same time, no amount of agreements or formal vows can change the fact that one day you may wake up as a different version of yourself, no longer as the inflamed personality who participated in making such agreements. As always, trust the guidance of your inner wisdom to determine which relationships feel supportive and which vows are meant to be released.

When a relationship reaches a point of completion, there may be a feeling of guilt for no longer desiring to be in such a partnership as if you do not have the right to make a new decision or fearing a Universe looking down on you for wanting something different. While this can become a chance to recognize guilt as the next one to be loved, it cannot replace the bold series of choices that only you can prevent yourself from making. For those in a conscious relationship, partnership, or marriage, the deepest commitment is to wake up each day and say, "Today I am not who I used to be. I'm a brand-new version of myself that only today can inspire. In this brand-new moment, I choose you again for whatever the day may bring."

This helps you build a relationship with your current reality instead of being shackled by the past. If there comes a time where you sense a journey with another has come to an end, it can only be the wisdom of the Universe guiding you forward into greater chapters of growth and expansion. This allows you to embrace every person much more deeply since the time spent together is so precious and uncertain. From this space, every relationship becomes an intimate expression of love in action. It invites connections to be rekindled in every breath, inspiring you to consciously participate in the relationships that you agree to be in.

As you awaken, the importance of conscious relationships becomes a pivotal focal point. Such relationships come to life when agreements are made heart-to-heart instead of negotiated by ego. When agreements are no longer rooted in obligation, scarcity, fear, or coercion, you bring to life a timeless remembrance of the infinite choices that are always available.

From one moment to the next, you are free to make choices in the name of love to discover the joy that you were always meant to find.

A Monk on a Mountaintop Meditating

In honor of the agreements and vows you have successfully cleared, I'd like to share a memory that came to me one day from a past life as a monk. I was shown a vision, as palpable as any object I can touch in this reality, of myself as a monk meditating on a mountaintop. During this meditation, I had a sensation inside my body that told me, "I am seconds away from experiencing nirvana." For a monk, nirvana is regarded as the absolute realization and embodiment of truth, the highest of all spiritual attainments.

As I sensed the impending arrival of nirvana, I was shaking while trying to hold my focus as I waited for my graduation ceremony to dawn. Just as nirvana opened up, my physical body as a monk dissolved.

I immediately entered the light and returned to Source. This is what many descriptions of heaven or afterlife are referencing. I remember being so confused as I left my body. I began speaking to an angel who was there guiding me back. I asked, "I was just about to reach nirvana. Why couldn't I have stayed moments longer?" I was so frustrated. The angel looked at me and said, "You would have always felt as if you were seconds away from nirvana. You would have been stuck in that moment of anticipation until the end of time."

When I asked the angel to explain more, he said, "You will always feel as if you are fingertips away from nirvana or moments away from your graduation because you were under the impression that you were something other than the Universe attempting to be completed. Can you see that you've been in nirvana all along, experiencing life as a person meditating or a monk in pursuit of it?"

As those words were spoken, the truth was revealed on a cosmic level. I watched myself from an omnipotent view on holographic screens. I was shown flashbacks of my entire life that led to becoming a monk. I saw images of being raised in an abusive household where my personality became inflamed in an attempt to match the egos around me. I became aware of the unconscious agreement I was making, which was "Maybe if I become more like them, I'll be spared more often."

As I lived in that abusive household making agreements from the negotiating standpoint of ego, I was hoping for mercy and to be spared from the abuse I had experienced. When I was of an age to care for myself in my late teens, I sought refuge in a monastery. As a way of trying to erase the memories and identity of being victimized by an abusive family, I took on the formal vows of a monk.

In accepting such vows, I felt relief from the victimized inflammation of ego. From that viewpoint, I could see how I didn't actually escape ego but reshaped it into a new spiritual character. By no fault of my own, I went from victimized inflammation into a higher state of righteous inflammation. I could also see how that wasn't a mistake of any kind. It was the necessary step in my journey that couldn't have unfolded any other way. I watched as each of those events led me exactly where I needed to be—sitting atop a mountain seconds away from nirvana.

As I watched that lifetime, I realized the vows and agreements that I made, while wonderfully pertinent, vital, and essential at the time, were no longer valid beyond that point. In many cases, the catalysts that inspired clarity and relief at one level of consciousness became the very things that I outgrew as a way of going even farther.

When I look back on that particular lifetime, on all of the agreements that I made with an abusive family, I saw that my way of being loved was to be abused less often. During times of abuse, the agreements I made were very valid for my survival. Even taking on the vows as a monk was essential to free me of the identity of victimhood, even if only to exchange it for a more spiritually sophisticated identity.

As this vision ended, it was clear that I would no longer make agreements out of obligation or vows from a space of fear. I would make inspired, heartfelt choices rooted in the freedom of love.

The most surprising part of all was as I gave myself permission to choose, I recognized the reclaiming of my power as the most primal fear I was meant to confront. Like so many energetically sensitive beings, in the end, you're not actually afraid of things lurking in darkness, but intimidated by the light and power of your own divine authority.

You may think you are afraid of insurmountable odds or the inevitability of loss, but perhaps the real fear is confronting and accepting how brightly you shine.

When you stand tall in the supreme radiance of your innocent nature, letting freedom choose what only love can embrace, there are no obligations or motivations of guilt. There is only the will to be what you're meant to become as a gift for all who appear before you.

Mastering Relationships

EVEN AFTER YOU REALIZE that you are the entire Universe playing in physical form, with others doing the same, the play still continues. We're not here to end the play but to transform it into higher vibrations of consciousness. As the play expands, it provides everyone greater permission to envision the greatest dream they were born to live out.

As you give yourself the love that only you can provide, you begin to notice how the more profound levels of spiritual evolution occur through the mastering of relationships. This includes the relationship between the mind and heart, which is reflected through the bond of a parent and their inner child. Additionally, it includes the mastering of the relationship between self and subject through your perception of a world around you.

When all of the interactions you have with your family, friends, or in your workplace become opportunities to serve our awakening humanity, a master of relationships has been found. No longer can you be satisfied by being enlightened in private and inflamed in public, knowing that every moment of conflict is an opportunity to discover the invaluable gifts that life provides.

It can be understandably difficult to engage in conversations and try to come from the purest state of love when you are around people who are not necessarily rooted in a similar vibration.

Those who are on different wavelengths of consciousness may not be interested in the things that appeal to you or may be unwilling to give you the same amount of time that you are giving them. Perhaps they are unwilling or unable to give you the same level of patience you are offering them. Maybe they're not as interested in knowing your life as you are in knowing theirs. They may not even be interested in knowing the depths of the spiritual journey that you're so excited to discuss. When finding yourself in those types of situations, it can be difficult to consciously engage with others who operate from such a different standpoint.

With love as your guide, you can be inspired to communicate in a way that brings your most treasured gifts to the surface, no longer waiting for others to be on the same spiritual page in order to show how much you care.

At a subconscious level, the way others interact with you does not determine the quality of your experiences. Rather, the quality of your encounters is based on how freely you give or how much you withhold. This means your experience of discord with another is not actually based on what they seem to offer or take away from you but what you are offering or withholding from them.

As you are willing to give more love, not less, even in the presence of behavior that you might think does not necessarily deserve such a gift, you can choose to engage in the most spiritually relevant and noble way.

When someone says words that may not feel good in your body, seem sarcastic in tone, and are meant to judge versus uplift you, this only offers you greater opportunities to raise the vibration of your response.

By responding to anyone's criticism with love, compassion, and acceptance, you are stepping forward as a master of relationships to create your own experiences, which has nothing to do with how anyone treats you.

In the most revolutionary way, you come to realize that your experience is only defined by how you respond to others, as powerful seeds are planted for their journey ahead.

The Healing Power of a Compliment

Even when meeting someone in their lowest moment of shame, desperation, or peril, you can always support that person's evolution and create a more enjoyable experience without negotiating with their inflamed personality. With love leading the way, you no longer require others to change in order to provide you with an uplifting experience, nor do you need to lower your vibration to match their energy until they evolve.

This is precisely the invaluable insight I learned as loving what arises transformed each of my relationships and interactions. I realized that each of us is a carrier of a unique vibrational frequency that only we can bring to the world.

The way in which we can transmit this energy is through the offering of a *compliment*. While complimenting can be misused in society and trivialized as a way of manipulating others to give you what you want, the spiritual purpose of a compliment acts as a selfless blessing of appreciation that reminds others how much they are valued.

Perhaps one of the most spiritually relevant practices is offering this type of genuine compliment to everyone you meet, even if you're interacting with someone whose beliefs or demeanor differs from yours. Even just by offering a brief moment of eye contact and a smile, you are transmitting your unique vibrational frequency to enhance their experience. Whomever you are meant to interact with is life's way of reminding you who is next in line to receive such a gift.

Perhaps as compliments, attention, and support are offered, you become the one who tells others what they've been waiting so long to hear. From that space, you help to free another heart from a history of pain, while providing a unique frequency of consciousness that no one else can transmit.

Turn It into a Gift

One of the most common themes I have seen throughout all stages of spiritual development is a tendency to be awake in private and inflamed in public. This can influence energetically sensitive beings to stay secluded at home or entrenched in spiritual communities, while withdrawing from the world in view. Hiding from the world is mostly due to not knowing how to respond to the unresolved debris sensed in the energy fields of others.

On a subconscious level, when you do not know how to respond to the words and actions of others, you unknowingly lower your vibration to match their energy. This is done in an attempt to become a mirror of their consciousness, hoping they will view you as an equal, so you can be spared of their pain, persecution, or abuse.

The question is, How do you interact with a person, no matter where they are in their journey, without lowering the standard of your experience to match them in energetic defense? The answer is in learning how to communicate through the act of complimenting in a process I call *turn it into a gift*. I discovered this process during a rather intense conversation that spontaneously revealed creative new ways to love what arises.

A few years ago, I was working with a naturopathic doctor to detoxify my organs. I soon realized my healing session had transitioned into listening to this doctor share her beliefs on spiritual superstitions, fear, and conspiracy theories.

As I relaxed into listening, I saw that while this person was open to spiritual matters and likely had had some powerful experiences, her overstimulated nervous system hadn't yet been addressed.

It was as if her ego was fully intact and decorated with an endless array of spiritual beliefs—with greater enemies to overcome, larger battles to conquer, and bigger concerns to anticipate. As she was talking about the potential downfall of humanity, I simply listened without a need to disagree with anything she said. As she spoke, I noticed how quickly and shallowly she was breathing. In response, I began breathing more slowly.

After she'd riled herself up into such a fearful frenzy, I could have justifiably interrupted and said, "I don't wish to speak about such negative, fear-based things during my appointment." Doing so would have created division between us and not have provided the opportunity to inspire and uplift her journey. I knew that while she was behaving from a state of inflammation, she was only here to be loved.

My challenge in the moment was to communicate without correcting her or matching her victimized, needy, and righteous inflammation. Because an ego cannot be content to solely make a point, it always needs to recruit other people into its agenda. She then asked me, "What do you think?"

I paused, took a breath, and allowed love to speak. I said, "It's obvious that you're very passionate about this subject matter. The fact that you're sharing with me what is so important to you allows me to feel more connected to you than ever before. Thank you for this gift."

She was completely stunned. I wasn't trying to stifle her; she just didn't know what to say. There was a ten-second pause of uninterrupted eye contact. As she resumed her role as the doctor in my appointment, she never mentioned anything fearful again.

Another example of *turn it into a gift* occurred in a mall when I ran into a friend I hadn't seen in more than ten years. The first thing my friend said to me was, "Looks like you've gained about ten pounds!"

In that moment I realized, *Here is another opportunity to turn into a gift.*

With the utmost sincerity of heart, I said, "You're right. I have gained about ten pounds, and the fact that you're bringing it to my attention lets me know that you must really care about my well-being. With you as my witness, I declare a renewed faith in making my health a higher priority. As I vow to become healthier than ever before and shed this excess weight, I'll make sure to keep you regularly updated on my progress since you seem so interested. Thank you for your support. What a gift it is for me. I really feel as if what you said is going to help me out."

He looked at me in a really surprised way, and I could tell he was thinking, *I didn't mean it as a compliment!* Of course, I knew his words weren't spoken with care and concern, but I chose to take it as a compliment and turn it into a gift that I offered in return. No matter the circumstance, love can withstand any type of judgment or ridicule and turn it into something more redeeming as a gift for every heart.

Whether you think others deserve your compliments or not, your ability to respond more graciously to them becomes the determining factor in enjoying your experience, regardless of the characters you encounter. When others judge, persecute, and lash out, it reminds you how often their innocence gets ignored. While their actions show you where they are in their evolution, that creates an opportunity for you to give them a gift they aren't able to give themselves. When the unconscious actions of others inspire you to *turn it into a gift,* you access the power of a true heartfelt compliment to transform reality with elegance and grace.

Cultivating Authenticity

Sometimes when I teach the practice of *turn it into a gift,* there can be a sense of discord arising within the inflamed personality that complimenting others is sure to dissolve. For some, it's as if giving a compliment to someone who is not treating you well somehow calls your own integrity into question. For example, you may find yourself asking, "How could I compliment someone when it doesn't feel authentic to offer such praise?"

Authenticity emanates from the subconscious mind. As I described earlier, the subconscious mind has two basic categories—familiar and foreign. When something new is brought into your energy field, the sense of *this doesn't feel authentic* is felt because it's something that your subconscious mind hasn't logged into your history of experiences.

When a particular experience falls under the category of foreign, your body is typically not given permission to resonate with it. Sometimes, the *turn it into a gift* teaching can get caught in the filter of your subconscious mind, causing you to say, "Because I don't have a history of doing this regularly and it wasn't modeled to me at a young age, it feels unfamiliar. My body is not resonating with it, and that makes me feel as if it's something that won't be helpful."

In your subconscious mind, it may be more familiar to defend or deny when people are unkind. When a heart-centered teaching like this comes along that invites you to love in response to personal turmoil, there can be a question of authenticity. One heartfelt compliment at a time, you are rewriting your subconscious mind to see every experience that comes your way as an opportunity to open up instead of shut down, withdraw, or lash out. All too often, shutting down occurs to protect yourself when under attack or in pain. While the hope of such a defensive position is to avoid more conflict or stress, it is important to remember that love is not a defensive energy. It is an offensive energy that only has gifts to share.

Through loving what arises, you start to realize that your daily practice of giving deeper eye contact, smiling to those who pass by, embracing yourself more often while turning anything that comes your way into a gift reveals the highest form of heart-centered joy. As an evolving master stepping forward into a new spiritual paradigm, you realize that all the wisdom you've collected in the privacy of your own journey is meant to be demonstrated as contributions for all. As that occurs, you are able to support the expansion of others, without their unconscious behavior undermining the quality of your experience.

When the question of authenticity is merely a matter of exposing your subconscious mind to a new series of inspired choices, you help to fulfill every prayer, dream, and desire by bringing love to life throughout each interaction.

No matter how hurt or disappointed you are in the behavior of others, it is your willingness to turn anything that someone gives you into a gift that liberates you from the despair of human suffering. At that very moment, there are endless gifts residing in your heart. You are here, exploring an evolving world that is ready to receive the miracle of your immaculate grace. How you decide to deliver each healing gift is entirely up to you.

The Merging of Mind and Heart

WHAT WOULD IT BE LIKE if you could go about your life, whether there is turmoil or harmony, without being limited by your experience of others? Instead of apologizing to someone for their experience or being in constant need of rescuing them, it is far more essential to honor your innocence as a way of inspiring relief in every direction. As your mind and heart unite as one, the more you see others beyond their divided unconscious states. This invites patience, acceptance, forgiveness, and compassion to become cornerstones of your encounters, no matter how inflamed anyone seems to be.

Whether as the activity of the mind or as reactive patterns in your body, loving what arises gives you full permission to be in a world without being victimized by the characters you see. As your mind and heart merge together, the comings and goings of life tend to lighten up. What used to bring disappointment and make it easy to lose all hope in humanity have become moments to cultivate an even higher vibrational frequency than ever before. As your vibration skyrockets, one inspired heartfelt choice at a time, your evolving perception of life expands the world around you.

No matter where you go, the world has been designed by the Universe to remind you when it's time to love your heart. Despite the circumstances at hand, your experience reveals the innocence of a child crying out for the reassurance, support, and attention of a loving parent who could only be found wherever you stand.

The Mind and Heart: A Union of Emotional Oneness

As the mind and heart come together in a union of emotional oneness, it informs the Universe that you are ready to explore the interconnection of all, as the eternal one I AM. Often referred to as self-realization, each glimpse of awakening allows you to experience the joy, sovereignty, and transcendence of viewing life through the eyes of the Universe. Perhaps such a universal view is already here. Maybe it's merely waiting for your heart to open so you can witness firsthand a truth that only you are destined to see.

While masquerading as the antics of an overstimulated nervous system, your true nature is a seed of consciousness that can often express itself in childlike ways. This is why I refer to it as your true innocent nature. Through each and every response, your childlike nature invites you to cherish the majestic wonder of your heart, just as a parent embraces their own child. As you develop an active connection with your innocence, you engage in a dialogue within the highest levels of unity consciousness.

As the mind and heart reunite in holy matrimony, you are able to see how everything that comes your way can be turned into a gift, and with greater receptivity and ease, you can cultivate love in every encounter.

However, when the personality gets inflamed, the eternal truth of consciousness fractures to divide emotional oneness into two seemingly separate parts: an overthinking parentlike mind, along with a cautious, innocent, vulnerable childlike heart. Even so, as the overstimulated nervous system unravels, the division between your mind and heart dissolves.

This process is much like a parent getting reacquainted with their own vulnerability by watching their child explore life for the very first time. The parent begins living vicariously through their child to reexperience things from a renewed perspective. Simultaneously, the child receives the attention, care, and protection they need to open up and grow to full potential.

Both child and parent are aspects of consciousness that come to terms with one another as your heart begins to open. When this occurs, it creates an environment in which you can return to your true nature as the light of divinity in form.

From a unified space of heart-centered mastery, you can be for everyone you encounter the parent they never knew, the best friend they forgot they had, and a transmission of grace they may not have known was here to be received. Once the truth of life's timeless beauty has been discovered, it flows through you to awaken the consciousness of all who come your way.

To unravel the overstimulated nervous system to the point where such a deep recognition can occur, your innocence brings to mind all the things you may have judged about yourself or others or that you experienced others judging about you. One moment of connection at a time, your childlike heart takes you through your own initiation into unconditional love as the most direct means to awaken the master within you.

Loving the one who judges or has been judged by others ensures that your innocence has your absolute trust, no matter what it says or requests. Throughout this process, the recurring theme is reminding your innocence of the support, understanding, and attention you are always here to provide. Over a period of time, your consistent attentive actions reassure your innocence that you are not going to treat it the same way it was mistreated by characters from the past.

As your initiation is completed to earn back the faith and trust of your true innocent nature, you emerge as the wise guardian of your radiant childlike heart. You may not always say "yes" to its impulsive demands, but you always know each request is not the purpose of each dialogue. Rather, each interaction between parent and child is rooted in love, as the Universe celebrates its long-awaited destiny throughout the heart-centered awakening of every being.

The Art of Self-Compliment

In the same way you have learned to do for others, you can meet the innocence within you and turn anything it says into the gift of a compliment as well.

Perhaps you've had experiences of fear, sadness, or anger and wondered how to respond in an authentic complimentary way. While it's natural to respond to fear by focusing on how to get away from it, you may not realize that any attempt to pull away from emotions only sends another message of abandonment to your heart.

Maybe when you felt sadness you've wondered, *How do I cure myself of sadness? How do I overcome it?* Such questions can leave you feeling quite defeated until you realize that sadness wasn't created to be overcome. To overcome sadness is to push away your innocence until it begins to act more "appropriately." Just like fear, moments of sadness cannot be defeated, cured, or overcome. They can only be transformed through your willingness to love. By learning how to support the one who is afraid, sad, or even angry, you heal each layer of conditioning as you change your relationship with the feelings that cannot be controlled or denied.

In the process of responding to these emotions through the art of self-compliment, you come face-to-face with all of the layers of conditioning within you. When the childlike heart brings you fear, sadness, and anger, the deepest wisdom within you can be inspired to respond in a complimentary fashion as a way of letting your heart know each emotion is safe to feel. Through the power of compliments, you focus your attention on the most redeeming qualities of each feeling. As you learn to respond to difficult emotions by finding the gift in each one—even the most tumultuous, frightening, or painful experience—you discover a more intimate way of living in harmony with the flow of life.

For example, when you experience a moment of fear, I invite you to activate the art of self-compliment by repeating the following healing mantra to your heart:

It's okay that you're afraid. The fact that you're
afraid is letting me know that you wish to
avoid a particular experience. I also know
that whenever you're afraid, this is a chance
for me to ask if you're using fear to get my
own attention or as a way of informing me to
venture in a different direction. No matter what
is revealed, fear is offering me a chance to be
clearer in the way the Universe guides me while
honoring the chance to love you, my innocent
heart, as never before. What a gift you've given
me. Thank you.

When you offer yourself the respect to welcome inner guidance instead of trying to be in charge of guiding your journey
forward, the clearest, most direct answers can be realized.
Whether fear is trying to tell you what not to do in any
moment or is simply attempting to get your attention, it can
always be met with the gift of unwavering support.

Feel what happens when fear is complimented and
acknowledged. No matter how intense it seems, even fear is
an expression of the Divine and not something to be overlooked, ignored, ridiculed, or denied.

When sadness arises, it can become an opportunity for love
to activate the art of self-compliment by saying to your heart:

I welcome your sadness. I wish for you to share
with me everything you feel about it even if
it's due to a loss of something that you weren't
ready to let go of. No matter how sad you feel,

these feelings just show me how meaningful things are to you. When you're sad because of loss or things that change, it shows me how deeply you appreciate what has been given to you and how much you value the gifts that come your way. I find that quality admirable and courageous.

Similarly, when anger erupts, frightening you with the magnitude of your own power, you can breathe slowly and allow love in by saying to your heart:

Hello, anger. I want you to know that you have a right to be upset. You are free to express in this way. I invite you to be upset for as long as you wish. You are free to point your finger at anyone you please and plead your case. I am listening to you. I acknowledge and compliment you because you respond so quickly to the actions of another who is not measuring up to your standard of conduct. Even though you are pointing your finger as a way of dealing with feeling disappointed, it just lets me know how high your values are.

Underneath the surface, the values that you embody enable you to point out disappointment and injustice in others. This shows me how eager you are to act as my protector even though I really don't need to be protected. Thank you for always looking out for me. As a result, you tend to get angry when things don't go my way or when others don't measure up to certain levels of expectation. You have the right to be heard, and you will not be punished, no matter what you think or say. I want to hear everything you wish to share, including every insult and judgment against those who persecute or judge. No matter how explosive you seem to be, I'm always here to listen, admire, and welcome you as the eternal one I AM.

Through these examples, you see how natural it can be to openly meet such intense emotions that may have distracted you in the past. By celebrating the vulnerability of your child-like heart, you discover the true purpose of compliments as a way of transforming whatever arises with love, acceptance, and authenticity.

From this space, the heart of surrender reaches an exciting point of completion as you ascend into the next level of spiritual growth and energetic expansion.

Conscious Communication

AS THE HEART of surrender is completed, you continue with your journey by discovering the skill of conscious communication. It is the next stage in mastering relationships that allows you to focus on the gifts you are delivering to others, instead of waiting for others to provide the attention, support, and care they may unknowingly withhold from themselves.

The reason you appear to live in a world among many others is because the recurring benchmark in spiritual evolution is noticing how well you communicate. No matter how anyone chooses to express themselves with you, your response reflects how open your heart tends to be. As the wise parent-like mind and the innocent childlike heart are reunited, love emerges to the forefront of your daily encounters to speak on your behalf. While you will still be the one responding, it may feel as if your words are emanating from a deeper, richer, and more inspired state of being.

A true enlightened master in a modern-day era knows how to communicate the love of their true self by translating it into a language that anyone can interpret. As you become aware of the skills and capabilities of a masterful conscious communicator, you are able to enhance your relationships, savor each encounter, and cherish any experience no matter the circumstances.

The reason communication is such an essential skill to master is because it is where most misunderstandings can occur. When there is an inability to consciously communicate, you may feel misunderstood by those around you, which can cause your heart to feel less inclined to open up at full capacity.

Mastering the Skill of Listening

Conscious communication begins with mastering the skill of listening. When listening, you give others a chance to be on the receiving end of your loving attention, which allows their subconscious mind to match your vibration.

While there are many evolving spiritual masters who yearn to wake up so deeply that they'll be able to levitate, walk through walls, or shape shift, one of the most impressive demonstrations of awakened consciousness is the ability to listen. An awakened being knows listening to be the most direct way to remind someone of their highest value. Whether lost in the beauty of a lover or exchanging smiles with a neighbor, the gift of your attention remains an extraordinary treasure you are capable of offering just by observing the innocence around you.

Have you ever acknowledged the power contained in your loving gaze? Have you seen how quickly and effortlessly everything falls into place when you accept that everything is here to be blessed by the grace of your attention?

Once you realize this, the activity of witnessing the transformation of all occurs by allowing others to be heard. When you are listening, you are no longer focused on what you think about things, or how they've been labeled, but on honoring the unique way such divine works of art have come to appear.

From this depth of awareness, you free yourself from needing to constantly prepare or rehearse your responses to what others are saying since a greater willingness to listen to them is one of the most loving ways to engage. This means you don't need to know the answers to anyone's questions, including your own, since the best answer is taking a greater interest in the questioner.

How profoundly would your life change if you no longer had to answer your own concerns or solve anyone's problems? What if you simply listened and gave loving attention to whatever comes your way?

An overstimulated nervous system doesn't allow you to listen without an agenda since it causes you to feel as if you are someone who is unsupported, overlooked, and misunderstood on a regular basis. This is often why human beings wrestle for control in conversations or find the time to debate one another. If consumed in ego, it's easy to feel as if no one is listening to you no matter how much attention has been given. Whenever you are in constant need of being heard, there is no ability to hear others or realize that you are the only one who can give yourself the attention your heart desires.

When anyone fails to give themselves the attention they seek, a feeling of being unsupported or misunderstood permeates their interactions. As that occurs, they can be motivated to recruit others to provide the attention they deny themselves. When two people come together in an attempt to get each other to offer a depth of approval that only comes from within, neither is listening to the other. This is how conflict is created. In conflict, the end result is propelling the overstimulated nervous system into greater momentum.

On the other hand, when two beings view conversations as a way of gifting their own heart with undivided attention, by practicing to be a better listener to others, there is no need for conflict to erupt. This is because both are aware of the fact that they are the only ones who are in need of hearing whatever they have to say. When human interactions become a way of practicing self-acceptance by treating others with more patience, kindness, and respect, a constant need to be heard shifts into listening as an act of love.

It is important to remember that your heart doesn't know the difference between you listening to others and others listening to you. The more openly you listen, the more accepted your heart tends to feel. As long as you develop the skill of listening, your heart feels safe to be open even if others lash out in defense.

Listening as an Act of Self-Love

When listening becomes an act of self-love, a stunning truth is discovered. In ego, it is common to believe that someone else's words or behavior is the reason you feel unaccepted, judged, or rejected. In reality, other people cannot affect you. It only seems as if they limit your experience when you refuse to hear a point of view that doesn't match your own. The more you allow yourself to listen, whether you agree with anyone's ideas or not, the less likely you feel rejected in the presence of another. The catalyst of rejection is life's way of reminding you how other people are not always created to treat you better than you treat yourself. Instead, they help you practice treating yourself better by how lovingly you interact with them.

This doesn't mean you should pretend to enjoy the company of those who treat you poorly. Instead, it invites you to cultivate greater compassion for yourself by allowing others to speak their mind. As the skill of listening is mastered, every heart is healed by the brightness of your being. When others have the right to speak, you inspire everyone around you to shine their light.

The Link between Attention Span and Listening

Throughout my work as an empath, I began to see how important the role of listening plays. I would notice people from so many different spiritual paths seeking my guidance mainly to resolve a feeling of being lost, disconnected from Source, or wanting to know what to do with their life. Even though I gave intuitive answers on every conceivable subject matter, it didn't seem to cut to the core of the issues. This challenged me to further explore why human beings felt that way. Soon enough, the answer became surprisingly clear.

Anytime a human being feels lost, disconnected, or unaware of what to do with their life, those feelings act as a feedback mechanism from the nervous system. They reflect the degree to which a person can become a better listener. Just as in breathing, when one listens shallowly, their love for themselves and others is conditional and shrouded in the stickiness of personal agenda. As the skill of listening expands, the feedback of being lost, disconnected, or without direction begins to dissolve.

While many sought my intuitive guidance, hoping I would know something they didn't, it wasn't the true reason why life had brought us together. The reason they were there was to learn how to listen, more deeply than anyone else had ever heard them before. As I helped others learn how to intimately listen to themselves, I discovered the mysterious link between listening and the nervous system.

I had already seen how listening remained shallow when a nervous system was overstimulated and deepened as it unraveled, but what was the link between the two? The link is your attention span. A short attention span indicates how overstimulated a nervous system happens to be. When the nervous system is overstimulated, you are bound to feel unsafe in your body, unsupported by the world, lost, disconnected, unable to make wise, decisive choices, and without direction in your life. As the nervous system unwinds, your attention expands to dissolve self-doubt, to enhance your interest in listening, and to guide you toward the most inspired choices that are always in reach.

One of the primary reasons a teacher offers spoken teachings of wisdom is because the act of listening lengthens your attention span. As it is lengthened, the body relaxes to invite your heart to feel safe enough to open. When attention expands, you are liberated from the core of human conflict.

No matter which character appears in your reality, each person is healed and returned to their original form just by giving them permission to speak.

When your nervous system is overstimulated, you aren't able to hear the extent of what anyone is saying. You might hear the first three or four words that remind you of associations to other things. While the overstimulated nervous system often causes you to quickly respond and share what the other person's words have inspired, it can get in the way of allowing another to be heard.

There can also be a tendency to interrupt others to correct how they see you. If lost in ego, it can be difficult to spend quality time with someone who doesn't perceive you the way you want to be seen. When you are driven by an agenda to be viewed in a certain way, you are unable to hold a space for anyone's heart to heal.

As a remedy, it is important to remember that how others view you is never about you at all. While they can share their views and opinions about who you are in their play, it doesn't have to match up with who you know yourself to be.

No matter the conclusions that others suggest when looking in your direction, each of their ideas represents outdated clusters of cellular debris being purged out of their field. This means that when it is time for others to purge patterns of judgment, the innocence of your loving heart may inspire their harshest criticism to be spoken. Despite what is said, that cannot lower your vibration or affect your energy field unless you agree to be the character they have imagined.

In most cases, it's not necessary that you even respond to those who are asking you to listen, simply because listening itself is already the best answer. Despite how judgmental anyone seems to be, your ability to let them be heard enables their innocence to feel important, cherished, and supported. Even if they don't seem to be transformed as a result of your listening, you are always the one who exits each encounter more expanded and evolved than any moment before.

As others are speaking out the clusters of cellular debris released from their nervous system, you can use that as an opportunity to offer full eye contact and listen with renewed heartfelt interest. From that space, you can notice that when people are inflamed, the speed of their words will match the shallowness of their breath. As you slow your breath to hold space as an active listener, the more your energy field expands to raise your vibration.

By elevating your vibration, you send a message to the other person's subconscious mind to acknowledge the energetic difference between you. In response, their subconscious mind will do whatever is necessary to raise their vibration in an attempt to match yours. This is how you are able to help pull other people up to a higher level of consciousness instead of lowering the standard of your energy to match where they are.

Through a more sincere willingness to listen, you are freed of a tendency to match another person's vibration or interrupt someone before they're done speaking. Often, interrupting someone in the middle of their sharing slows the healing already in progress.

It may feel distinctive to make a "better point" or correct their misperceptions, but to interrupt them equally reveals the overstimulation of your nervous system. This is why the most heart-centered approach is to hold a sacred space for both hearts to heal through the practice of conscious communication. Otherwise, a spontaneous moment of healing can quickly escalate into a shouting match in which two people fight to have the final word while the innocence of both hearts gets ignored once again.

Offering Advice, Interrupting, and Lashing Out

As a lightbearer of heart-centered consciousness, you are always in a position to hold sacred space for life's deepest healing. When a desire to interrupt becomes an opportunity to slow your breathing and listen at a more intimate level, you increase the likelihood of the other person being more open to receiving what you have to say, once you've allowed them to make their point.

Even after someone has stated their case, you may experience the ways in which others are unwilling or unable to be as masterful of a listener as you are for them. As tempting as it might seem to point out how faithfully you've listened or how unfair it is that they're not giving you the same in return, it is far more beneficial to acknowledge any degree of frustration or your disappointment as the next ones in line to be loved.

Even though an act of engaged listening may increase the likelihood of someone reciprocating the same interest in return, it cannot be guaranteed to unfold in any way other than to inspire your most profound healing.

Conscious communication levels the playing field of your daily interactions by reminding you of the ways in which listening to others offers you the chance to practice being a better listener to yourself. No matter how one-sided conversations seem to be, they can always feel fair, adequate, and equitable, as long as listening is viewed as an active meditative practice. Even when a willingness to listen inspires a response, whatever you wish to say out loud is not necessarily what they need to hear or absorb. In many cases, your response to others reveals the messages of inner guidance that only you need to hear from yourself.

When overlooking that truth, you may find yourself in situations where the righteous inflammation of ego causes you to draw from your favorite spiritual insights in an attempt to educate those who seem misinformed. By projecting your advice onto others, conversations can quickly become heated debates when the greatest advice you know is ignored or rejected. And yet, conscious communication will remind you, time and time again, the one who speaks is primarily the one needing to hear the words they say.

The fact that you are in a position to hear them out offers you more opportunities to practice being a better listener by holding a more conscious space than they may ever be able to hold for you.

When your heart has been put in charge of how you respond, you can see that you're motivated only to give advice to another to remind yourself of the next important step for you to take in your life. Even if the advice you are eager to offer another person matches the actions you've already implemented in your life, the fact that you are inspired to impart such wisdom motivates you to act upon it on a more consistent basis with renewed enthusiasm.

As you learn to communicate consciously, you recognize the willingness to show greater interest in the uniqueness of another as one of the powerful gifts you can provide. Through a renewed commitment to listen in a more engaged way, you offer the innocence of others the chance to purge all they are willing to release through the words they are motivated to speak. Anything you would need to say to correct their assumptions, judgments, opinions, or conclusions offers you the chance to speak out loud the words you need to hear and to become more aware of the action steps that are pivotal for you to implement.

Even though you are interacting in a world of others, the relationship with your true innocent nature masquerades through ongoing interactions with various characters. This doesn't mean the way that others behave is a reflection of a behavior within you. It is more the case of meeting the emotional disposition of another as a reflection of times in your life when such behavior offered you less love from others, instead of more. It's as if your history of life experiences is cross-referenced by categories of emotions. Any unresolved feelings that linger in your cellular memory take shape and form as the temperament of other people.

While the words they share with you represent the purging of cellular debris from their energy field, they also represent aspects of your past that await the support, attention, and encouragement that seemed to be missing from your past.

This is precisely why listening to others acts as a chance to practice listening to your innocence at a more intimate level. Even if the person speaking asks for advice, you can ask yourself the question, "What are the words I always wanted to hear whenever I felt that way?" The words that would have made a difference, if only those in your life had known what to say, become the gifts you are here to offer as a way of healing both hearts.

In conscious communication, the way someone else acts, behaves, or speaks to you cannot justify matching their unconscious behavior and lashing out at them. Even if you were to lash out, you can notice this as an opportunity to take some private time to slow your breath, to actively engage with your inner child, and to listen to whatever your heart wants to say. This can include offering love to the aspect of self that lashes out at other people as if they are a sibling who gets all of your attention. No matter how frustrated you are in the presence of another, you are only crying out for your own loving approval, despite how much attention you believe another person owes you.

If there are words that others did not say that you wanted to hear, then they become your brand-new personal love statement that can be spoken to yourself as often as necessary.

One inspired choice at a time, you increase the likelihood of having a positive experience with anyone you meet. No longer will the conditions of their ego limit your reality because only your choices and perceptions can determine the quality of your experience.

A Willingness to Be Honest

The cornerstone of conscious communication is a willingness to be honest. The importance of honesty cuts to the core of how much you have placed all your faith in the greater cosmic picture of the Universe. While so many people know that life has a bigger role for each of us, the only way to demonstrate, anchor, embody, and trust in life's supreme plan is to be totally honest.

When you are honest, you honor whatever response comes as a result of your most authentic sharing. Despite how drastically the snow globe of your reality might get shaken up, this only occurs in order to guide your journey in an exciting new direction. In time, you may see how this redirection was always meant to guide you into a far greater reality than you may ever have found without trusting the perfection of the Universe.

One moment of honesty at a time, you allow the precision of life to swiftly deliver you into the paradise of your highest destiny. In order for such a destiny to unfold in the most elegant and miraculous way, it is important to allow the wisdom of your heart to become your inner compass. When you are willing to speak your highest truth in the presence of another with the utmost love and compassion, it demonstrates how much you trust your divine guidance to reveal the exact words you need to hear.

If through your honesty, you end up losing opportunities or relationships, those may appear to be worst-case scenarios when you are attached to outcomes that differ from life's supreme plan. Even when the odds seem stacked against you, that could only be a brand-new chapter of growth and expansion revealing itself out of the ashes of what you thought was supposed to occur.

The Integrity of Honesty

Before you can be honest in the presence of another, it is essential to learn how to be honest with yourself. This requires a courageous depth of integrity to become aware of how you want others to treat you, so that you can be that way for others whether or not they're able to do so in return for you.

As a way of understanding what it means to live in integrity, you can ask yourself the following questions: "How would I like someone to listen to me when I am in the depths of turmoil or writhing in pain? If I had something to say, how would I want others to listen as a way of helping me to feel heard, nurtured, and cherished?"

Whatever comes to mind in response to these questions becomes the gifts of integrity that you are destined to provide to others. This can help you uncover the true meaning of integrity as a willingness to act, speak, engage, and listen in exactly the way that you would want anyone else to be with you. By maintaining integrity as a conscious communicator, you always create opportunities for everyone to evolve, even if the behavior of others does not meet the standards of your values. Even when it's your turn to speak, integrity invites you to declare, in the presence of others, your unwavering trust in the supreme plan of the Universe by how passionate, transparent, and honest you're willing to be.

The Healing Practice of Frequency Matching

Whether between friends, coworkers, lovers, or parents and children, there is an energetic practice, called *frequency matching,* that can inspire more conscious communication. Regardless of the type of relationship, frequency matching establishes an agreement that whenever one person feels unheard or disconnected, it invites both hearts to work together to find a common vibration.

As part of this practice, either partner has the right to say, "I'm feeling disconnected from your heart," or "I'm having a hard time connecting with you."

In response to this feedback, both partners engage in frequency matching by holding hands while looking into each other's eyes. The objective is to match each slow inhale and exhale of your partner so both are breathing at the same relaxed and gentle pace at the same time. As both partners align their breath for a minute or more, a common vibrational frequency allows their hearts to entrain and feel supported so that deeper conversations can resume.

As a healing exercise to help you open to the practice of frequency matching, you can look into a mirror and take a few moments to gaze into your own eyes. If you find it difficult to make full eye contact with yourself, simply slow your breath and look for as long as you can. The point isn't to resist blinking or to gaze with any strain, but to open up to a more fulfilling connection with your innocence by facing yourself directly.

The more often you face yourself, the easier it is to welcome the vulnerability of others without a fear of being hurt or rejected. Expanding the potential of any personal encounter always begins by establishing a more intimate relationship with your heart. Through slower breaths, engaged listening, repeating your personal love statement, complimenting your innocence, and being more honest with yourself than ever before, you become the first person you are sure to heal as a way of inviting your light to shine.

From this space of vibrational alignment, relationships become the redeemer of truth and the transformer of victimhood. No matter how misunderstood you seem to feel, you can infuse any experience with heart-centered consciousness simply by choosing a more inspired way to respond.

The Importance of Slowing Down

WHETHER AS A CATALYST for awakening or as a way of discovering the passion, happiness, inspiration, and excitement dwelling within you, each spiritual aspiration is fulfilled by cultivating greater integrity with your heart, which begins by slowing down the pace of your life.

It is natural to feel hesitant about approaching your life in a more relaxed and gentle way. When run by an inflamed personality, it can be easy to believe that the best opportunities may pass you by if you don't do everything in your power to keep up. In a world where people have been conditioned to accomplish tasks by any means necessary, the purpose of your journey is to learn how to be as aligned with spirit, as you are inspired, thriving, and productive.

Whether you discover an unshakable desire to live more mindfully or find yourself exhausted by the demands of each day, life will unfold in a way that guarantees the growth and expansion of your highest evolution. If the way you are living is out of harmony with your natural state of being, the Universe may create unexpected shifts in your circumstances as a way of interrupting the chaos of your momentum. As a result, you will be slowed down by the perfection of grace until you are able to welcome each experience with kindness, humility, and appreciation.

As slowing down occurs, you will find yourself more spiritually aligned with the flow of the Universe, so you can take your time with each step forward. This helps you make more inspired, heartfelt decisions while growing in a way that allows your innocence to feel safe.

Living Your Life at a Slower Speed

Cultivating integrity with your heart is a decision to live in a more relaxed, conscious, and heart-centered manner. While it may come naturally for some, for others it's a necessary way of proving how impossible it is to miss opportunities you are destined to encounter. Since you cannot miss out on experiences that you are always meant to have, every breath offers you the chance to put your faith into the hands of the Universe to remember how blessed, supported, and divinely guided you already are.

It may be difficult to imagine a trusting Universe or to know how much you matter when living at a frenetic pace. Once you slow down, something more than the ups and downs of personal gain and loss can shine through. A clear sign that you are becoming more aligned with your heart is a feeling of relaxation. When relaxation is felt, it reveals your true masterful ability to be in tune with the flow of the Universe while also being an active participant throughout your day.

Relaxation is always the preferred rate of speed for any level of spiritual exploration. Anytime you rush through your journey, direct experiences of transcendence are replaced with shallow degrees of understanding. Because certain stages of awakening can drastically slow down the pace of your life to nearly a standstill, the Universe often prepares you for such a path by making it nearly impossible to keep moving at an unconscious speed.

When a feeling of relaxation seems regularly absent from your activities, this is a sign to make the necessary changes to slow down and lighten the load of your schedule. Not only is slowing down essential for merging your mind and heart as one, but also for the benefit of a spiritual journey you may not have realized you were already on. It may come as no surprise that when loving what arises, more relaxation enters your field of experience. This invites your heart to feel safe enough to open as relaxation confirms how aligned and balanced you have come to be. Whether your goals are spiritual, personal, or professional in nature, you can no longer fool yourself into thinking how much more relaxed you'll feel once you have earned a certain achievement, especially if the way in which you approach each task pulls you out of balance along the way.

As relaxation indicates that you are successfully maintaining integrity with your heart, your nervous system unravels to free you from the heaviness of guilt, shame, fear, victimhood, and obligation. When you slow down and relax into a more natural rate of speed, you create the perfect climate for life's most incredible discoveries to unfold.

When relaxation becomes your doorway of awakening, you discover a more honest relationship with life. Instead of dragging your innocence along for the ego's adventure, you are guided to soften into each breath so your mind and heart can be on the same page. As a way of integrating this truth, I invite you to repeat the following healing mantra:

> I acknowledge that it is essential for the evolution of my being to slow down the pace of my life, no matter the pressures that call out for my attention. In support of my highest evolution, I accept that life will create whatever reality is necessary to give me countless opportunities to reunite with my heart. As I slow down, I welcome the choices that only my heart knows are aligned with the highest perfection of the Universe. In discovering my heart as the home I never left, I allow my true innocent nature to feel safe enough to merge into the light of my being, as the love that I am.

Honoring the Speed Limit of the Heart

It can be quite exciting to discover the magic and miracles that surface when living in integrity with your heart. Whether you notice this as a perfect assembly of synchronicities, an increased flow of intuitive guidance, or even the ability to manifest help and resources from others before you even ask, a remarkable version of life dawns once relaxation has inspired you to move at a more conscious rate of speed. This allows each task to become an ongoing practice of energetic alignment.

While success in many areas of life may be contingent upon getting things done, the rewards of spiritual evolution are discovered when the way you approach each task is equally as important as the goal at hand.

When you are able to be relaxed during your daily activities, your heart tends to open more freely. This allows your mind to rest in a natural state of silence so you can focus on being as thoughtful and caring as you are driven to thrive and succeed. Even when you notice how tense, rigid, frustrated, or short-tempered you seem to be, this can only be a reminder to slow down into a more harmonious flow.

In every chapter of your life, there is no wrongdoing or mistakes to confess. There are merely opportunities to notice suffering, stress, judgment, aggression, or pain as signs to balance your assertiveness with heart-centered care.

When your most profound spiritual adventure is decorated as the comings and goings of everyday life, each task becomes a chance to work in harmony with the Universe in a more thoughtful and courageous way. This makes it essential to view your heart as the speedometer of your energy field, whether at work, in your personal relationships, or throughout your spiritual path.

By living at the speed of heart-centered consciousness, you are able to make peace with your inner child once and for all. When the importance of being relaxed is as essential as the goals pursued, your heart is able to feel safe throughout the duration of each encounter. If relaxation seems absent from your experiences, it becomes a signal to slow down the pace of your life by loving what arises.

One "I love you" at a time, you invite greater support from the Universe so you can celebrate each moment with everything to welcome and nothing more to prove.

No Longer Speaking the Words
That Hurt You the Most

Another essential step in cultivating integrity with your heart occurs through the exploration of an important question. Similar to your personal love statement, this question can bring greater healing into your life.

With the utmost honesty and compassion, ask your innocence, "What are the words that you remember that hurt you the most?"

Perhaps those were the words or phrases you heard that created the greatest amount of pain, devastation, and disappointment for you earlier in your life. Please do not justify or try to explain why those words were spoken to you. This is an opportunity to transform any lingering traumas by remembering the most hurtful words that shaped your sense of self in such a painful and limiting way. As those words bubble up to the surface, a new level of healing is ushered in by giving a voice to the pain and disappointment that has gone unrecognized for far too long.

Maybe they were such as: "Not now, honey, don't bother me. Please go away, I can't deal with you right now. You're too much for me. You weren't supposed to be here. It's your fault. You were a mistake. I don't know how to love you. You made me do it. You're annoying me. Please stop talking."

Whatever the most painful words were, your adult mind doesn't have to rationalize what may feel so painful for your heart to remember.

As you explore the most hurtful words that were ever spoken to you, it is understandable to feel blame, anger, and resentment toward those who spoke them to you. If this rings true for your experience, always know that you can hold a space for healing to occur by allowing your innocence to speak the words it never had a chance to say in response to such hurtful interactions. In order for the most profound transformation to unfold, a voice must be given to your pain to express honestly toward your perpetrators from the past. While those may not be words you are likely to speak publicly, speaking them allows a voiceless, suppressed, and victimized innocence to finally be heard. Whether expressed in the form of a letter that you shred or delete upon completion, an art project conveying pent-up feelings, or singing aloud the words you never got a chance to say to the person who hurt you, true healing often occurs by providing a platform of self-expression for the aspect of self that felt it never had a choice or a say in the matter.

Because you are consciously allowing such words to be spoken, without needing to specifically address the particular person in question, there is no judgment occurring. With every sincere expression that doesn't have to involve anyone else directly, more space opens up to inspire your own heart to open.

Once you have made contact with the phrases that have affected you in the most painful way, another important step in cultivating integrity with your heart is vowing to never speak those words to yourself or anyone else again. While each memory celebrates a moment in time that you were always powerful enough to survive, the most profound form of spiritual redemption is breaking the cycle of cruelty by no longer passing along the hurtful words that were ever spoken to you.

Loving what arises is not only rooted in saying the words you've always wanted to hear, but also in eliminating from your vocabulary the words that were so painfully remembered from the past. When you are willing to spare yourself and others from the phrases that caused such pain and despair, you are beginning to view life through the eyes of the Universe where the vulnerability of all can be embraced as One.

From this space, the mastery of relationships is no longer such an unattainable goal, but the most natural way of interacting with life.

Making Peace with Your Inner Child

It can be nearly instinctive to dwell on the cruel words others have passed along to you when further healing is required. Perhaps the painful words or actions of others can only affect your experience when you either match another person's vibration of insensitivity or refuse to be more loving toward the one who lashes out. Whether you are able to welcome life from a spiritually aligned perspective or get triggered by the actions of others, the most important thing is making peace with your inner child.

When rooted in heart-centered consciousness, your innocence interprets the world as a reflection of your patience, kindness, and care no matter how unconscious anyone seems to behave.

One of the most direct ways to make peace with your inner child is to communicate with it on a regular basis. Whether it is repeating your personal love statement throughout the day or finding a quiet space to silently allow your innocence to speak the unfiltered words it was never able to say in the past or saying "I love yous" to your heart, you are able to resolve every point of contention by becoming the acceptance and support that others haven't provided you.

Another way of making peace with your inner child is by no longer defining your sense of worth or measuring your spiritual progress by the actions of others. While we are One in our essence, we are unique as individuals.

By supporting the aspects of yourself that have never been heard, respected, accepted, or adored, you invite the highest intelligence within you to emerge. As your inner child is honored and respected as the form through which the Universe is revealed, you are guided through every twist and turn with harmony, peace, ease, and joy.

When not engaging your innocence with the attentiveness that a loving parent offers a child or the respect of honoring that child as the wisdom of the Universe, you unknowingly remain at odds with your heart, which amplifies the noise in your mind. Since your mind tends to be as noisy as your heart is closed, making peace with your innocence remains paramount to the evolution of your being.

To make peace with your inner child once and for all, please repeat the following healing mantra:

> Dearest inner child, I'm so sorry if you've felt
> ignored, abandoned, ridiculed, or denied in
> any way. I'm sorry that anyone has ever hurt
> you. I'm sorry if I have put you in a position
> to be around those who threatened your safety,
> unaware of your experience, while I attempted

to be fed by those I now realize were never designed or destined to fulfill me.

I apologize if your pleas for my attention were overlooked, ignored, or misinterpreted as symptoms that I must fight, clear, dismantle, or transcend throughout my life. I see that whether disguised as my personal assistant, my imaginary guardian, or the insistent life coach who lives in my head, you were only attempting to capture my attention just so you, my beloved heart, could spend some more time with me.

I'm so sorry you've had to work this hard. I accept that the pain of my life is not based on the circumstances I face, or determined by what I think I lose, or rectified by what I gain, but on how out of alignment I am in loving you the way you deserve to be loved. I apologize for how often I rush through life without keeping in mind the rate of speed that makes you feel safe.

As of this moment I vow to love, honor, and adore you as never before and to regularly speak the words that you have always wanted to hear. Even if they are words you've already heard, I will speak them more often with renewed passion and enthusiasm. And the words that were so painful for you to hear, from whoever shaped your reality from the past, will no longer be words I say to you or anyone else. From now on, I realize that what I speak to another is a love letter sent to you, my sweet inner child.

I want to let you know that even though it looks like I'm talking to others in the world, I am not denying you in any way. When I am acknowledging you, all things are healed. When I am cherishing others, it is you I am honoring.

I acknowledge you, my inner child, as the vulnerability of my heart and the center of my Universe. I welcome my highest destiny as a way of honoring and celebrating you, the most important and crucial element in my journey. From this moment forward, I will carry you with me wherever we go, together as One, for the well-being and liberation of all.

My dearest inner child, I want you to be a more active part of my life. I need you to help me complete my journey. You have an important role to play. If you open up and accept this moment as a new beginning in our relationship, I will love you as you were always meant to be loved. As I affirm your important role throughout my evolution, you will no longer have to work so hard to fight for my loving attention, acceptance, and approval.

As of this moment, I surrender to love by letting you lead the way. I love you.

Whether these words inspire a new beginning within you or continue to crack apart the density that can no longer divide you from your heart, it is your willingness to be in tune with your true innocent nature that sets the stage for life's profound miracles to be revealed.

11

Everything Is Significant

AS GREATER COMMUNICATION is established with your inner child, the mind and heart merge so that you can remember your eternal nature once and for all. As everything is met with relaxed heartfelt focus, you begin to see how quickly things can transform. Just by bringing a more engaged attention to the circumstances in view, you are becoming an open window of divinity that invites the winds of change to heal everything in sight.

Beauty: The Divine Nature of Love

The natural impulse of love is to acknowledge the existence of divinity in all. When love recognizes its divine origin, this is known as beauty. While it is common to associate such a word with attractive physical characteristics, recognizing beauty in this new way honors a moment in time in which the divinity of One discovers the truth of all in another.

The more often you view your life through the eyes of divinity, the more beautiful you tend to feel. This may help you see the truth of beauty as a spiritual acknowledgment of cosmic innocence in physical form.

The more openhearted, gentle, and innocent anyone tends to be, the more beautiful they appear. Even when the ups and downs of life have overwhelmed the lives of those around you, the ugliness of their cruel behavior helps you acknowledge someone who is desperate to be supported and encouraged at a more intimate level. Instead of trying to change someone's experience or imposing spiritual ideas onto others, you can invite the beauty and innocence of their divine nature out of hiding just by reaching out in a more thoughtful way.

If you already see the innocence in others and beauty in the world, this simply acknowledges how spiritually aligned you already are. Once this level of alignment is active in you, I invite you to take it even one step further by turning your instinctive awareness into an inspired spiritual practice so even those who hide their innocence behind defenses, pain, criticism, and selfishness can remember how beautiful they were always created to be.

Just by catching a glimpse of something that passes you by, you are acknowledging the innocence and beauty of its existence, simply by allowing it to come into view. This is the gift of *significance*. Whenever life is honored with significance, every person, place, and thing can be celebrated for the vital and equal role it plays throughout the divine plan. Since everything is composed of matter, the consciousness within each form remembers how important it is—when invited to be seen. As you realize the powerful gift of significance that can be offered to the world, the beauty and innocence of all begins to shine through at a more accelerated rate.

Perhaps the characters around you are more likely to treat you with respect and honor your divinity when they are offered the gift of your loving approval. What if your waiting for a person's behavior to change before taking the time to cherish their existence is precisely why they lash out? In *the love revolution*, a tendency to withhold attention fuels the flames of personal conflict, whereas loving the hearts in view invites something deeper to the surface. This doesn't excuse cruel behavior or justify toxic relationships in any way. Providing you are in a safe environment that does not threaten your innocence, it is your willingness to witness and speak to the beauty of all that reveals a truth beyond description.

If, however, you find yourself regularly threatened, dominated, betrayed, manipulated, or abused by others, you can honor their innocence, as well as your own, by removing yourself from volatile environments. Without anyone to control or hurt, a more potent healing journey can unfold once another person's cruelty is no longer distracted by the radiance of your being.

Becoming Rooted in the Body

From a spiritual standpoint, love is an instinctive act of acknowledging something as divine in nature, no matter how it may appear to you. When such a depth of truth has dawned in your heart, everything will be recognized in this beautifully breathtaking way. This includes an understanding that any moment you fail to see the divine origin of anyone is the exact moment that life invites you to stop and remember what is divine about you.

One way to remember the nature of your divinity is by offering more significant attention to the parts of yourself that may often go overlooked. The more often your body is cherished and adored, the faster it transforms.

What if you began referring to your body as beautiful, no matter how it functions, has been judged by others, or has been perceived by you? Just by saying "Hello, beautiful," you're not only creating a greater connection between the mind and heart but celebrating the truth of your body as divinity in form.

Since your body is the Universe, you can greet each part with "Hello, beautiful" as a way of sending infinite blessings and waves of healing energy to every corner of the cosmos.

If you notice any kind of embarrassment bubbling up when saying "Hello, beautiful," this is an unsuspecting sign of spiritual evolution. From a cosmic perspective, the awareness of embarrassment represents the mask of ego cracking apart. Even though it might feel intense or uncomfortable, the presence of shyness or embarrassment confirms how courageously your innocence is attempting to open up.

Can you sense a difference in how relaxed you feel when showing renewed interest in your hands, organs, legs, fingers, or other parts of your body? Notice how each part is committed to maneuvering you through time and space to serve the joy of your highest destiny. As each part plays a significant role in your journey, why not take a moment to say "Hello, beautiful" to it? Beyond the immediate sensation of shyness or embarrassment, you may notice how extraordinarily whole you become when all parts of yourself are equally acknowledged.

This also sends an important message to your innocence that frees it from creating problems or imbalances just to be on the receiving end of your loving attention. When we were children, it might have been common to have felt the most kindness and care from others when we were sick or in pain. That often can create a subconscious belief that invites the body to manifest pain or illness as a way of inviting a greater connection with those we love. The majority of illness and physical pain acts as critical stages of spiritual growth, where the physical body takes the time to catch up and become more aligned with the rapidly expanding consciousness of the soul. It's amazing to see how more healthy, aligned, and balanced you can be whenever loving attention is freely offered on an unconditional basis.

It's not as if someone with an illness should cause you to think, *They must not love themselves enough.* That would be an unfortunate judgment projected upon someone whose innocence needs more support and encouragement through critical stages of growth and expansion. And yet, when loving what arises is a way of supporting yourself, throughout each gain and loss, your body no longer has to use imbalance or desperate behavior as a way of seeking the power of your approval.

When you acknowledge yourself with "Hello, beautiful," you're informing your heart that it no longer has to create problems, manifest dramas, or sabotage any aspect of your life in order to earn the attention that you can freely provide. Whether as a way of greeting your innocence in the morning, acknowledging the efforts of your body at the end of the day, complimenting yourself regularly, or giving blessings you share with others, "Hello, beautiful" remains an effective way to bring forth a new spiritual paradigm that inspires the world to heal.

This is what it means to start your own *love revolution.* It is discovering the courage, passion, and desire to reveal your divine qualities, incredible talents, and remarkable abilities for the benefit of all—at the rate in which loving yourself becomes your most deliberate spiritual practice.

Pain and Illness as Catalysts for Transformation

While it might seem easier to love your heart once you feel safe in your body, it is taking the time to connect with your innocence that allows true safety to be found. There are two crucial ways to help you feel safely rooted in your body no matter what you encounter throughout life. The first is always being honest with yourself by admitting how you feel. When lost in ego, it can seem difficult to come to terms with your feelings and easy to point the finger of blame at circumstances that seem to get in your way. As you wake up, you recognize each perceived obstacle, setback, and distraction as a cleverly orchestrated catalyst of transformation created to ensure your highest evolution. One of the more revered and yet misunderstood divine catalysts is the sensation of pain.

Pain, whether arising as physical, mental, or emotional discomfort, acts as the recurring signal of an ever-expanding consciousness. No matter how uncomfortable or inconvenient it seems, the intensity you feel confirms that an important transformation is taking place. Because of how unexpected, stressful, and tumultuous such moments of expansion can be, it is quite normal to make an attempt to fight, avoid, or ignore the pain you're in or seek out remedies to make the pain subside. Even so, I am not suggesting that you pretend to enjoy the pain you're in, but that you open up to the healing effects it is sure to provide.

As a catalyst of divine will, part of pain's role is to make you more honest with yourself about the things you can't control. It is a faithful agent of truth that resurfaces in life to help you become more open, receptive, and vulnerable instead of fearful, desperate, and defeated.

If pain were to have its way, you might acknowledge moments of difficulty by allowing yourself to admit, "I'm in so much pain right now, and I don't know what to do."

You might confess, "I'm in absolute pain right now, and I hate every minute of it."

Surprisingly, your innocence won't feel rejected as long as you are being honest about your circumstances. Your inner child only tends to feel rejected when you either move away from pain or blame yourself for it. In fact, the more transparent you are with yourself, whether pain is present or not, the more your innocence develops a voice that allows your heart to open.

While it's easy to believe how much more open your heart would be if you weren't in so much pain, a more fundamental truth can be discovered once you stop fighting against the forces of nature that inspire greater honesty. Even if you were to say, "I despise this pain," you are confessing the truth of your experience with conscious intention. It doesn't have to be eloquent or projected onto others—it just needs to be the most sincere confession you've ever made.

Once pain has invited a greater depth of honesty to the surface, perhaps the next step is acknowledging the one who doesn't like to be in pain as the next one in line to be loved. If you're not ready for such a step, you can just admit how you feel. It may require you to admit, "I hate this pain so much. All I care about is making it go away."

Whatever is true in your experience, the most loving response is resting in the grace of honesty to give yourself space to heal until something deeper opens up. One honest confession at a time, you are able to relax in the presence of pain so you can honor the one who resents the experiences they cannot control or avoid. Just as you've learned to do with difficult emotions, each moment of adversity becomes an opportunity to breathe slowly into the center of it, which allows everything around the pain to soften and relax.

Whether overwhelmed by pain, frustrated by circumstances, or coming out on the other side of a tumultuous healing journey, the transformative power of pain offers you full permission to be honest with yourself as a way of accelerating the process. As always, before you can cultivate the integrity to be open with others, you must first be honest with yourself. When you open up to honesty, your innocence always feels safe and secure, no matter how much discomfort there may be.

Whether healing righteous, victimized, entitled, or needy inflammation out of your energy field, the ego often maintains a position of insisting, "It's not fair." While it's normal to sense a lack of fairness when facing a pain that cannot be controlled, this reveals a timeless opportunity to grow, expand, and evolve beyond the limitations of conditional existence.

As that occurs, you won't just be on your best behavior as long as everything goes your way or traumatized when unexpected circumstances come into view. Instead, there is a more intimate flow of perfection that carries you beyond every breakdown to discover an inner radiance that shines as the brightness of all.

Embracing Confusion

The second way to be safely rooted in your body is by embracing confusion as an unlikely ally. Often when confusion is experienced, it is interpreted as a sign of needing to seek out clarity, healing, and resolution. Through the eyes of the Universe, confusion is not the opposite of clarity but a gateway into the greatest wisdom ever known. Confusion occurs when all of your preconceived ideas, definitions, and reference points get displaced.

If your life were a metaphor of a book, then confusion would be the spontaneous ability to lose your place in the story with a renewed interest in venturing forward without attachment to previous chapters. Because losing your place in your personal story is precisely the way that deeper discoveries come to life, confusion is not something to fix or avoid in any way. Rather, it is the very space in which your greatest awakenings are revealed.

In the blink of an eye, you may find yourself suddenly astonished by the actions of another, not realizing that they have been placed in your reality in order to bring confusion to the forefront of your experience. If embraced as a divine catalyst of growth and expansion, you can allow confusion to help you lose track of grudges that you've been carrying from the past.

While the strategy of using confusion as a tool for growth is simple, it's not always easy or comfortable to experience. With love as your guide, you can embrace confusion, not as something to understand, but as a space void of any understanding whatsoever.

For some, having nothing to understand can feel intimidating or unsafe. Yet, if you relax into not needing anything to conclude, figure out, or keep straight, your consciousness expands to see how everything is known *for* you—not *by* you. This doesn't mean you are refusing to understand, but rather that you are transitioning into allowing understanding to *find you*, instead of you pursuing it on a regular basis. This means you will always know everything you need to know, at exactly the moment you need to know it.

In the beginning stages of a spiritual journey, your progress is determined by how much more you understand. In the higher stages of evolution, progress can be recognized by how much of your gathered understanding has been integrated. The more wisdom integrates, the more it seems to vanish from your memory. It's as if the Universe inspires moments of confusion to remind you what is no longer needed to be known as you round the corner into newer chapters of evolution. Often, the understanding that brought so much comfort at an earlier chapter in your life becomes a new reference point for ego at a later stage.

As you venture into the less conceptual levels of spiritual growth, you will encounter recurring moments of confusion that free you of the memories, ideas, beliefs, and conclusions that bind you to an overstimulated nervous system. That occurs until your body has become an empty vessel for the vibration of love to shine through. Since love is the only thing confusion cannot take from you, it can be recognized as the only true understanding in existence.

Since it only helps you make room for love, it is your willingness to accept the true purpose of confusion that allows your heart to open. In order to embrace confusion as an unlikely ally, please repeat the following healing mantra:

> I acknowledge that whenever I'm confused,
> uncomfortable, feeling out of sorts, or mixed up,
> I accept confusion as an unlikely ally that is only
> here to help me lighten the load for my journey
> ahead. When I don't know where to go or what
> to do, and even when I don't know who I am or
> what I'm not, I remember that I always have the
> ability to relax into confusion to honor it as a
> divine catalyst of growth and expansion.

> No matter how confused I seem to be, I
> acknowledge that its intention is to help me
> forget what I thought I knew, as a way of
> integrating such wisdom, which creates space
> in my life to reveal an even greater truth.

> I hereby acknowledge confusion as a friend
> that could only be an enemy to righteousness,
> the shadow of victimhood, a nightmare to
> entitlement, and the greatest fear of neediness.

As I allow confusion to be embraced, I can be
honest about how confused I am and notice
that no amount of confusion prevents me from
relaxing—no matter the understanding only I
may think I need at the moment.

I allow confusion to assist in unwinding my
overstimulated nervous system so I may discover
the true safety that is always within me. By
slowing my breath and placing my hand on my
heart, I love the one who might not know how
powerful of a gift confusion can be.

When you are honest about your pain and willing to befriend
confusion under any circumstance, you have given the
Universe permission to guide you into the ever-revealing
nature of truth. It is a peaceful, clarifying, and harmonious
space of being, where love is the only answer to any question
imagined.

As you become more rooted in your body as a living
expression of heart-centered consciousness, you may notice
the Universe being as gentle with you as you have chosen to
be more soft and supportive of yourself.

Both pain and confusion are divine catalysts that I call "the
uninvited guests." This means they have a way of showing up
often at times you least expect or want them around. There
is something extraordinary you can learn by seeing how pain
and confusion always maintain their roles as uninvited guests.

As they show up in the most inconvenient of times and in
the most unlikely of places, you can develop a willingness to say:

While I did not invite confusion or pain into
this moment, they are here for an important
reason. In the name of befriending my
experience with greater integrity, I welcome
the uninvited guests that show up to ensure my
highest evolution.

As you acknowledge the experiences of pain and confusion, the only way for them to maintain their identities as uninvited guests is to move out of your field. In many instances, the catalysts you invite to stay seem to have somewhere else to be. Equally so, the ones you deny tend to stick around until they are welcomed.

When pain and confusion can be viewed as allies instead of enemies, you are able to feel safe in your body under any circumstance. No matter how confusing life seems to be, despite how much pain you happen to be in, or regardless of how many disappointments come your way, your innocence can feel cherished, honored, and supported every step of the way.

12

Awakening: What to Expect

DURING THIS PIVOTAL TIME in history, more and more people are experiencing spontaneous awakenings. Even if it appears that you live in a world in which so many characters are struggling to keep up with the perpetual demands of society or constantly looking for ways to speed themselves up, this is all an essential part of a greater divine plan. An overstimulated nervous system is much like a car engine. The faster you try to make it go, the higher the RPMs will rev, which inevitably results in the combustion of the engine. While you could conceivably live your life at such a frenetic pace, waiting for your nervous system to crack in order for consciousness to expand, loving what arises offers a far gentler and more direct way to enter the doorway of eternal freedom.

One way of understanding awakening is to examine the role of your nervous system. When put into overstimulation mode, at some point, it may "glitch" and cause the whole process to momentarily come to a halt. As that sudden stop occurs, your consciousness expands to your natural state of being, revealing a perspective that is in contrast to the way you have been conditioned to view life up to that point. The shock between these two extremes can generate serenity, euphoria, a feeling of intimidation, the anticipation of death, or even a sense of fear, as you are catapulted into a perception of reality you may have never noticed before.

When awakening dawns, and your mind is suddenly quiet, and you can feel everything in your body, which may include the ability to tune into the experience of others, there can be quite an adjustment process. Whether that creates excitement or fear in you, you may not be able to determine where you begin and others end. You may not know what to do with yourself, how to exist, or how to act without a character to portray. You may find yourself asking questions such as, "How do I talk like this? How do I choose like this? How do I go about my day playing a role that no longer seems to be who I am?"

When a spiritual phenomenon of this depth and magnitude occurs, it is very important to befriend confusion and to be honest about your pain so you don't misunderstand the opening of consciousness as something to resolve or turn away from. Befriending confusion will help you to see these experiences as an invitation to explore a reality beyond understanding. No matter how clarifying or confusing it may be, you can remain open and attune to an endless wellspring of joy, regardless of what is or isn't happening.

Whether these words are a foreshadowing of what will soon happen along your path or help you come to terms with what's already unfolding, your willingness to love what arises is an essential companion when traversing each stage of realization.

Even when all sense of who you thought you were dissolves and disappears, it is the perfection of love that propels you from one level to the next. With love as your guide, you are destined to be as integrated, compassionate, and wise as you are liberated, healed, reborn, and free. Even as awakening dawns and it seems as if there's no one left to be, this doesn't mean there is no one left to love. When the characters you've been playing suddenly disappear, love is always here to embrace itself as the One eternal heart masquerading throughout the bodies of all.

Whether the door of awakening has already been opened and you wish to bring this journey full circle or you're being prepared for the most miraculous adventure you may not understand, each fear, worry, and concern becomes your ongoing invitation to return to love. No matter your experience, perception, the beliefs you carry, or the identity that is no longer here, each auspicious moment of expansion allows life to be seen through eyes of the Universe to remember how equally everything matters.

The Natural Cycles of Expansion and Contraction

As you come to understand the spontaneous or gradual awakening of consciousness as a glitch occurring in the overstimulated nervous system, it can be helpful to explore in more depth the complexities of this miraculous adventure. When your consciousness expands, your nervous system might be initially unable to hold the vibration of this brand-new frequency. If this occurs, you may notice your nervous system regenerating patterns of overstimulation. It may seem as if your consciousness, that had been so expanded, begins to shut down and return to the behavior of the inflamed personality that your awakening seemed to have rescued you from.

When such expansion and clarity come crashing down, this can leave you feeling as if you're traveling backward in your spiritual evolution. During those times, it is important to realize no one is at fault. There is no need to blame yourself or anyone else for the natural progression of the way everything has been designed.

Throughout your awakening, you'll often get sneak previews of your newly expanded state of being as the Universe provides a taste of the way life will be on a recurring basis. And yet, when your nervous system cannot maintain that expanded energy, it will shut back down. As you return to your conditioned state, you have a chance to reexperience ego with greater consciousness. This helps you revisit unresolved patterns from a much clearer perspective.

Maybe more definitively than ever before, you start to see that everything exists as perfectly orchestrated catalysts to teach you something about yourself that you may not have known. Since nothing occurs by chance, no experience exists as an obstacle on your path. It could only be the next pearl of insight, merely appearing to be in your way as the most direct means to help you evolve.

Through a play of contrast, you awaken to an expanded level of consciousness and are able to notice how different things will be once your nervous system is able to hold such a vibration.

After the preview is complete, you are condensed back down into the inflamed personality of ego while rooted in a brand-new perspective. By oscillating back and forth between these states of expansion and contraction, you come to see what is exactly the same and unchanging between both extremes.

This is the silent inquiry of your ever-evolving spiritual journey. Whether you have already been freed of each reference point or eagerly await a permanent vacation from the inflammation of ego, it is an opportunity to recognize that both the one who is expanded and the one who is contracted are here to be loved.

Throughout the ups and downs of contraction and expansion, it's as if you are ping-ponging between those extremes to ensure your love becomes unconditional. On one end, everything seems joyous, perfectly in flow, and fulfilling at every turn. On the opposite side, everything feels unsafe, unsettled, and imbalanced as if nothing's right with the world. It is very natural to oscillate back and forth until enough momentum is built up to help you settle into the middle. It is here that both extremes collapse. There is neither a high nor a low; there is just reality being itself as radiant expressions of truth in action.

Kundalini and the Energetic Component of Awakening

While ping-ponging back and forth between the polarities, very unexplainable symptoms and experiences can occur. It can feel like electrical currents are surging through you as if various parts of your body are being struck by lightning. You might feel pressure at the base of your spine, activating the energetic component of spiritual evolution. It is often referred to as kundalini awakening where the energy rises up the spine like a snake uncoiling from the base of your tailbone. As it arises to open your chakras and activate the energy field of your body, the kundalini energy pushes out the cellular memory that does not match the vibration of consciousness awakening within you. It's as if the nervous system and kundalini energy work together as partners for the evolution of your journey.

In the beginning, the nervous system purges the initial layers of inflammation to prepare for the energetic component of awakening. When it arises, kundalini energy picks up where the nervous system left off to help release the additional layers of conditioning. Whether released out of your field by either the nervous system or kundalini energy, it may seem that as you awaken, you are triggered by people around you more often. As you've come to learn about uncomfortable emotions, whatever you're feeling, you are healing.

As triggered emotions are welcomed with more openness and receptivity, they are released to assist you in returning to Source. By loving every emotional outburst or at least loving the one experiencing it, you're clearing space within your field to assist the kundalini energy in ushering in a new heart-centered consciousness.

While you may want to hurry past the more tumultuous aspects of awakening, the slower you move through this stage, the faster you progress. As always, the most direct way to accelerate any spiritual process is by relaxing into it. When relaxation becomes another ally on your path, your heart can open to ground the surges of kundalini energy. If you're unable to relax, always return your attention to your inner child to discover the next one to be loved along the way.

The "Traffic Jam" of Cellular Memories

Sometimes as the kundalini energy rises, there can be a "traffic jam" when the cellular memories don't have enough momentum to leave as quickly as they're being released. This can manifest as physical illness, exhaustion, apathy, anger, or depression. In the new spiritual paradigm, illness is often recognized as an important sign of transformation already in progress. It is much like someone feeling the intense contractions of labor while not ever knowing they were pregnant.

Because illness can be a sign of massive energetic expansion occurring in your field, there is no need to blame yourself for it as if physical upheaval is proof of not having done your spiritual work properly.

Through the rapid energetic expansion of spiritual evolution, the old cellular memories are trying to leave and the emerging new energy becomes "jammed." This energetic traffic jam can cause your organs to become inflamed or imbalanced, creating the symptoms of physical disease as a way of showing you what needs more attention.

While the energetic aspects of awakening are not the sole explanation for illness, this is an opportunity to notice imbalances as a chance to be nutritionally congruent and attentive to the needs of your body. Whether you seek the help of a medical professional or an alternative health practitioner, the intention is to provide loving care to the parts of your body where symptoms are present. This allows the ecosystem of your energy field to work in greater harmony for the well-being of your journey.

I share these insights with you so that you are not alarmed or unkind to yourself if during your process of awakening, things are not always comfortable or convenient. By loving what arises, you place yourself in the most optimal position to welcome each experience with the greatest amount of faith, humility, and ease.

The Pitfalls of a Spiritual Ego

Throughout the process of awakening, it is common to have powerful openings that reveal miraculous truths about reality. While such experiences verify that you are going in the right direction, they can sometimes be misunderstood as endpoints along the way. While transcendent experiences validate your arrival into a new level of consciousness, it is vital to remember how any stage of awakening always foreshadows the next stage beyond it. When forgetting the infinite realms of realization, there can be a belief that your journey is complete. While patterns of desperation may no longer remain and you might find many symptoms fading into remission, this merely sets the stage for the next horizon of discovery on an endless trajectory of ever-revealing grace.

In the aftermath of such profound spiritual experiences, a new identity for the ego may emerge. This is where the righteousness of ego can become *spiritual righteousness.* It feeds itself by correcting the misperceptions of others based on the experiences it remembers having. This is when the victimhood of ego can become *spiritual victimhood,* begging a Universe to fulfill endless desires or blaming it for taking away its most prized experiences throughout the stages of expansion and contraction.

When ego is lost in spiritual victimhood, it may even look to the Universe in a superstitious manner, asking, "What do I need to do correctly to earn my way back into expansion?"

The entitlement of ego can also become *spiritual entitlement*. Based on who you have thought yourself to be, or even in the absence of the character you thought you were, it's easy to become spiritually entitled, as if your experiences somehow make you better than others. Instead of feeling inferior to others by comparison, you can come to believe you are spiritually superior. If this occurs, it's easy to lose sight of the humility that recognizes each person as a master in training.

Although we are all unique and deserve to be honored for the exquisite talents each of us can express, at our core, we are One, as the supreme reality of Spirit in form. This doesn't mean you shouldn't feel excited about a new consciousness waking up within you, but to remember how the uniqueness of your transformation foreshadows the same existential rites of passage arising in every heart.

Further, the neediness of ego can become *spiritual neediness*. It can masquerade as intense compulsions, such as always needing to raise your vibration, expand your attention, or be in charge of all that you are aware of. Here, you may find yourself constantly asking, "Am I seeing it right? Is this the clearest view? Do I need to make sure I'm not misperceiving?"

While raising your vibration, inquiring into a clearer view of reality, and even expanding your awareness can be wonderful ways to evolve, they cannot assist you in unearthing your greatest discovery if the ego is attempting to take charge of your journey. It is never a matter of whether you are doing the right things or doing things incorrectly, but noticing whether or not your behavior is coming from a space of relaxation or compulsion.

While a spiritual ego can use a collection of insights and experiences to create a new character to play, this new character cannot exist in the presence of love. It may even be cloaked in a charming persona as the defender of light against the evils of darkness, unaware that such a battle can only be waged between the extremes of spiritually based judgments.

A spiritual ego competes with love instead of cooperating with it. *To cooperate with love is to dissolve into the light of your being.* Spiritual egos overlook this step and cannot force it to occur even if there might be greater benefits to behold by trying to make it happen.

In many cases, a spiritual ego assumes that "who" it has become or the truths that it has realized are a replacement for heart-centered attention. The spiritual ego can insist it is beyond the need for love or judge it as a lesser play, existing only on the personal level of experience. Even if you have realized love to be who you are and have seen how the giver and receiver are actually one and the same, this doesn't stop the unfolding of love as an endless revelation of truth.

This helps you realize how spiritual discovery doesn't minimize the importance of love in any way. It clears out every distraction or misunderstanding so there is nothing in the way of loving yourself—no matter who you insist you are or aren't anymore. The further you explore the truth of existence, the more aligned in love you become.

In fact, the more transcendent an experience, the more willing you are to support your body, honor your personality, and admire the world as magnificent decorations of divinity.

Whether disguised as spiritual righteousness, victimhood, entitlement, or neediness, it is only the childlike heart masquerading as newly created spiritual personas that fight for the very attention that only you can offer. Even when you feel expanded, contracted, or somewhere in between, and no matter how often you meet your own liberation face-to-face, each moment inspires you to embody the highest vibration as a transmitter of heart-centered consciousness.

The Ultimate Surrender

As your awakening dawns, it is quite common for your experiences to seem less than the fairytale romance you may have hoped they would be. Instead of being immersed in never-ending bliss or having the ability to respond consciously in every interaction, there is a palpable emptiness that can make you feel quite helpless if you are without a clue as to what is going on.

When you wake up, your attachment to ego dissolves out of your energy field. As attachments to ego evaporate, you are suddenly unable to be fed by the people, places, and things that previously defined your existence.

In ego, it is easy to imagine the notion of caring as a response to the people, places, and things that feed your identity. That means as you wake up from the need to be fed, it can feel like you no longer know how to care about the things that used to be the center of your Universe.

Without a clear sense of knowing how to care, and in the absence of needing to be fed, your reality can quickly turn into a bleak and lifeless desert of personal boredom. Imagine: nothing that used to define you provides any surge of significance or fulfillment while your long-awaited new way of being has yet to be revealed. It's very much like an existential stage of purgatory. It's not as hellish as the pain you've known in the past, but it still feels miles and miles away from the heaven that seems anywhere else but here.

Some may continue to avoid this crucial stage of awakening by looking for new things to be fed by. When the ego looks for new things to feed its existence, the desire for more meaningful relationships is often where it places its focus. While everyone deserves to know the true joy of companionship and to be reunited with their soul family, it is common to desire these types of relationships above all else as a way of steering your attention away from the empty despair of spiritual-limbo land.

For those who are knee-deep in awakening, yearning to break through to the other side, but without a clue as to how to care about life when nothing seems to matter, I offer you this important exercise.

I invite you to sit comfortably, close your eyes, and repeat the following healing mantra:

> There is no way out of pain. There is no way out of judgment.

Without overanalyzing these phrases, the energy within them strips away the pretense of a spiritual ego in order to inspire a heartfelt surrender that gives every remaining option over to the hands of fate.

This is not a process that can be rushed or fast-tracked, although a healing mantra of this depth and magnitude has been created to give you the most direct access to a truth already alive within you. As you have come to realize, knowing yourself as a "fill-in-the-blank" spiritual concept cannot spare you from the sorrow of emptying out.

As you take a bold step in the direction of life's most heartfelt surrender, the acceptance that there is no way out of pain or judgment unravels every strategy of manipulation and avoidance. Without manipulation or avoidance as active forces in your energy field, your choices can now be arranged and orchestrated by the will of the Universe.

While I assure you there is a light at the end of the tunnel, it is your willingness to relinquish every morsel of expectation that allows the intelligence within you to redirect your consciousness in an exciting new direction.

Sometimes a belief that you know how the spiritual path is supposed to work or an insistence of having "already done it" all can block the recognition of your most profound insight. This insight is an acceptance that there is no way out of pain or judgment. As you relax into this healing mantra, you might be surprised to see how quickly your war against life comes to an end.

This doesn't mean you will always feel pain or be in judgment. Instead, pain or judgment will no longer be enemies, especially when any perceivable enemy is often a spiritual ally in disguise.

13

Ascension: Planetary Awakening

WHILE THE TERM *awakening* points to the concept of an individual journey of expanding consciousness, the term used to describe planetary awakening is *ascension*. As you assist in the evolution of our planet through a journey of spiritual growth, you will likely experience periods of profound expansion and contraction, shifting between extraordinary highs and infinite lows, until all polarities balance out. You may experience ringing in your ears, lightning bolts of electricity surging throughout your body, swirling energy emanating from the base of your spine, waves of anxiety, moments of existential bliss, feelings of impending doom, a desire to die, or even a sense of being reborn.

Throughout it all, you are destined to receive the revelation of life's eternal truth. In your own unique way, you are destined to remember the heaven that is already here as a love that has no end.

When you open up to such a timeless reality, you are able to experience life from an extraordinarily fresh perspective. From this view, the outcomes and circumstances that were once so important have now been replaced by a desire to master relationships, explore the art of communication, and love what arises.

As You Grow, the Planet Evolves

As your life is healed of the past and infused with renewed faith, joy, and enthusiasm, your heart can be recognized as the center of the Universe. With each "I love you" offered in response to anything you think, say, witness, or feel, the innocence of all is uplifted by the grace of your radiant eternal presence. As all beings are reborn and returned to their original form, a more spiritually aligned world reflects a new heart-centered consciousness that you were always destined to deliver into the world.

Whether you have just started to dip your toe into this profound spiritual odyssey or are using these words to guide your healing journey to a long-awaited point of integration, you are becoming aware of a greater purpose of being that all lifetimes celebrate and foreshadow. As you participate in the ascension of Earth, you may come to recognize your own personal evolution as the most direct way to elevate the consciousness of the world.

From that space, you are no longer a person waiting to be liberated by life. You are life's eternal liberator, setting free the truth in every heart by taking the time to love your heart more often.

The Slingshot Effect of Ascension

During this time of awakening, if you wish to explore the highest reality in existence or traverse the outer limits of the Universe, you build up the momentum to skyrocket across galaxies by staying grounded in your body. Being grounded is the ability to feel safe. Feeling safe occurs when your heart has opened. An open heart is the end result of providing the kindness, care, support, and attention that only you were designed to offer yourself.

No matter how often you seem lost in the ups and downs of circumstance, playing out the righteous, victimized, entitled, or needy inflammation of a human ego, you are the highest destiny of divinity, made manifest into form, as an evolving modern-day spiritual master. Whether you are attempting to restore order in your everyday life or trying to figure out a way to find joy and fulfillment wherever you go, each moment represents a timeless meeting where the light of your divinity encounters its innocent nature as a celebration of eternal love. As you bring kindness and care to your personal interactions, you are able to recognize the vulnerability within you as a collective outcry of an entire planet.

With love leading the way, an entire species no longer starves for attention and can usher in a spiritual renaissance of cosmic proportions.

As a way of anchoring this new vibration during the most exciting time in human history, please repeat the following healing mantra:

> I acknowledge throughout each feeling, thought, belief, and action that while my experience may

be rooted in an individual perspective, I accept that in reality I'm having an individual experience of what is unfolding throughout the totality of all.

I acknowledge that what appears to be an individual journey is an entire planet being collectively healed, awakened, and loved as I am.

I may perceive myself as an individual having a unique personal experience, but I am the *all that is* within it. While appearing human in form, I am experiencing the spiritual rebirth of an entire planet, which, in my experience, is depicted as the evolution of a person.

Even though each person demonstrates the ascension of an entire planet, I accept that there are other dimensions where the evolution of One is being experienced in slightly or even drastically different ways. This means I am not just awakening in one way—I am awakening in *all ways.* If I wish to explore the other parallel dimensions, where this one is embodying the ascension of a planet in infinite ways, I don't have to travel into outer space to discover those other dimensional versions; they are already here, decorated uniquely as other people.

I acknowledge everyone I see as the eternal One I AM. Even if it feels as if I'm only one among many, I accept this is merely one perspective within the vastness of infinite views. No matter how anything seems to be, I can rejoice that I am transforming this perspective for all, just by allowing it to be on the receiving end of my loving attention.

I also accept that others are here to transform additional aspects for my evolution as well. Together as One, we celebrate the victory that has already been ensured since the beginning of time for the liberation of all.

Through this transmission, you have been infused with the courage, passion, and clarity to boldly step forward into the world, inviting your heart to be the inner navigator that guides you beyond the boundaries of time and space. As you explore a world of endless potential, you are destined to remember love as the essential answer to any question or concern.

Throughout your journey, you are not discarding individuality in the name of unity. Rather, you are awakening the truth of unity by reuniting your mind and heart in holy matrimony. When mind and heart are one, you uniquely celebrate your spiritual evolution on instant replay as the growth and expansion of each individual.

Whatever Arises, Love That

During the most incredible time in Earth's history, you can support the expansion of consciousness by celebrating your innocence and cherishing the ones you love more than ever before. This is a time to speak to those you encounter as if it's the first time you have ever met. It's a chance to know that as an individual walking this Earth, the joy you are able to feel, the peace that emanates within you, the love you are here to cultivate, and the excitement you radiate give all beings greater access to the magnificence of their immaculate potential.

Now is the time to come out of hiding and let your voice be heard by confessing your true nature as the glory of divine innocence in human form. Whether you whisper silently into the vulnerability of your heart or shout at the top of your lungs from every rooftop, *you are the living proof that all is well.*

You are the source of life's eternal witnessing and the orchestrator ensuring that love always has the final word. As your evolution is revealed, there are four powerful words to carry with you wherever you go: *whatever arises, love that.*

As tendencies to fight, defend, and negotiate fall by the wayside, every layer of righteousness, victimhood, entitlement, and neediness dissolves out of your field. One auspicious moment at a time, an open heart gifts you with masterful relationships, artful communication, and an alignment of perfection that no limiting belief can ever comprehend.

While it may seem as if this is the end of our journey together, it could only be the beginning of a brand-new adventure. May all be blessed, uplifted, liberated, and reborn, now and forever, by the love that you are. And so it is.

Acknowledgments

THIS BOOK is dedicated to the innocence dwelling in every heart. May it act as a timeless reminder that you are never alone, that you are here for an important reason, and that soon your energetic sensitivities will be revealed as the greatest tool you've been given to assist in the evolution of this entire planet. Because everything is collaboration in consciousness, I would like to acknowledge those who were essential in helping me bring this book to life for the well-being of all who are meant to receive it.

First, I would like to thank Julie Dittmar for answering the inner calling that set us both on course to fulfill a destiny beyond anything either of us could have ever envisioned. Julie, "thank you" doesn't seem like quite enough to truly honor your dedication to these messages and your unwavering, heartfelt support. I am eternally grateful for your companionship and nurturing care throughout each awakening, upgrade, and integration. With each adventure, I rejoice in admiration and gratitude of the highest order for who you are in my life.

I would also like to thank my family for a lifetime of love and encouragement throughout my earliest years of growth and preparation. You have always been my biggest supporters, and I'm so thankful for how often you encouraged me to find my voice and share it with others.

A special thank you goes out to Tami Simon and everyone at Sounds True for their exquisite assistance in publishing this book. I have loved every moment of this process as well as the friendships that have blossomed along the way.

I thank my team of inner guidance that has been with me since my earliest memories, walking with me and holding my hand throughout each insight and revelation. You allowed me to make each decision while showing the way with the kindness, ease, precision, and grace that has become the standard for how I work with others.

And finally, to every member of the Love Revolution, spanning all corners of the globe, thank you for allowing me to be a part of your journey and for the teachings and transmissions of energy you continually inspire.

I see you. I love you. I am you.

Many blessings to all,
Matt

About the Author

MATT KAHN is a spiritual teacher and highly attuned empathic healer. His spontaneous awakenings arose from an out-of-body experience at age eight and through his direct experiences with Ascended Masters and Archangels throughout his life.

As an empath who uses his intuitive abilities of seeing, hearing, feeling, and direct knowing, Matt feels others' emotions and is able to pinpoint what blocks any heart from opening. He brings forth revolutionary teachings through both the written and spoken word that assist energetically sensitive beings in healing the body, awakening the soul, and transforming reality through the power of love.

Matt is a bridge between the mystical realms and the path of awakening; he inspires profound spiritual growth and life-changing energetic expansion in audiences worldwide. Many spiritual seekers have awakened to their true nature and have experienced amazing, unexplainable physical and emotional healings through Matt's profound and loving teachings and transmission of sacred heart wisdom.

For more information about Matt's teachings (or to book him for a speaking engagement); to order additional supportive audios and videos for your journey; or to attend an upcoming live event, Soul Gathering, or retreat, please visit truedivinenature.com.

About Sounds True

SOUNDS TRUE is a multimedia publisher whose mission is to inspire and support personal transformation and spiritual awakening. Founded in 1985 and located in Boulder, Colorado, we work with many of the leading spiritual teachers, thinkers, healers, and visionary artists of our time. We strive with every title to preserve the essential "living wisdom" of the author or artist. It is our goal to create products that not only provide information to a reader or listener, but that also embody the quality of a wisdom transmission.

For those seeking genuine transformation, Sounds True is your trusted partner. At SoundsTrue.com you will find a wealth of free resources to support your journey, including exclusive weekly audio interviews, free downloads, interactive learning tools, and other special savings on all our titles.

To learn more, please visit SoundsTrue.com/freegifts or call us toll free at 800-333-9185.